HARPER CHASE

Nefarious Crimes: Unsolved Murders Vol. 3

Contents

Introduction

In the eerie silence that shrouds unsolved crimes, there are narratives that resist the passage of time, echoing endlessly in the corridors of the unknown. This book invites you into a gripping exploration of some of the most bewildering and haunting unsolved murder cases, where every question beckons into deeper mysteries, and every answer seems just beyond reach. We embark on a chilling odyssey, navigating through tales that remain etched in the collective consciousness for their enigmatic nature and the unresolved agony they carry.

Our journey begins with the heartbreaking story of Emilie Meng, a young girl whose disappearance in Denmark sent shockwaves through a tranquil community. We then traverse the dark alleys of Washington D.C., exploring the enigmatic death of Seth Rich, a case mired in political intrigue and unanswered questions.

The double murder of Sydney Land and Nehemiah Kauffman in Las Vegas unfolds next, revealing a tale of love and loss under the city's bright lights. In the quiet town of Delphi, Indiana, the tragic fate of best friends Abigail Williams and Liberty German adds a haunting chapter to our exploration, their voices echoing from a chilling recording.

We venture into the affluent corridors of Toronto with the mysterious deaths of billionaires Barry and Honey Sherman, a case wrapped in a web of secrecy and complexity. The silent horror of the Winnipeg Serial Killings then leads us into the heart of Canada, where a predator's shadow looms large.

In each chapter, we confront the unknowns of cases like Dorothy Scott's disappearance, the bewildering findings in the Dean and Tina Clouse investigation, and the perplexing clues in the search for Chase Massner. We also delve into the past with the story of Carol Cole, unravel the tangled threads of the Keddie Murders, and seek answers in the haunting case of Brenda Gerow.

We reflect on the enduring impact these stories have on the human psyche. Each chapter not only unravels a narrative steeped in mystery but also serves as a somber reminder of the lives that were abruptly and tragically cut short. These cases, etched into the annals of true crime, stand as testaments to the undying human spirit's search for truth and justice. They are beacons, guiding us through the fog of the unknown, urging us to never cease our quest for answers in a world rife with unanswered questions.

Emilie Meng

The mysterious disappearance of Meng captivated the nation, unfolding like a perplexing thriller that began in the early hours of 10 July 2016. Meng, known for her vibrant presence and a cherished voice in her local church choir, was last seen in the quiet hours of the morning. She was making her way home on foot from Korsør Station, after a lively night out with friends in Slagelse. The group had arrived at the station around 4 a.m., and from there, Meng embarked on her journey home alone, a journey that would become a focal point of intrigue and concern.

What was expected to be a normal Sunday morning turned into a day of anxiety and uncertainty. Meng, who had a singing engagement at a local church at 9:30 a.m., never appeared. This uncharacteristic absence raised immediate alarms among her friends and family. The community quickly mobilized in response to her disappearance. A groundswell of volunteers joined forces with the police in a desperate search to find Meng. This wasn't just a small effort; it was a widespread, passionate endeavor that saw countless individuals combing through various locales, clinging onto hope.

The investigation into Meng's disappearance revealed a series of complex twists and turns. Several leads emerged, propelling the police towards three main suspects. Among them was a 33-year-old truck driver, whose life and activities became a subject of intense scrutiny. Another, a 67-year-old local, saw his house searched five times in a thorough quest for answers. Yet, despite these promising leads, the suspects were eventually released, deepening the mystery.

As the weeks turned into months, the police developed three main theories to explain Meng's disappearance: that she had chosen to run away, that she had been involved in an unfortunate accident, or, most ominously, that she had become the victim of a crime. Each theory opened up a multitude of possibilities, but none led to a definitive conclusion.

Throughout the 168 days of her disappearance, Meng's story was not forgotten. Volunteers, fueled by concern and solidarity, blanketed the nation with missing person posters. Their dedication was a testament to the impact Meng had on her community. These hundreds of volunteers, united in their cause, searched tirelessly for Meng, hoping for a resolution to the mystery that had so deeply affected them all.

The tragic tale of Meng's disappearance culminated in a heart-wrenching discovery on Christmas Eve, 24 December 2016. In a somber twist to the festive season, her body was found in the serene yet now poignant setting of a lake at Regnemarks Bakke near Borup, located in the tranquil Køge Municipality. This discovery transformed the serene landscape into a focal point of a dark mystery. The area, usually a place of natural beauty and tranquility, was suddenly besieged by police activity as authorities cordoned off the scene to conduct their meticulous investigations.

The following evening, in a somber press conference, the police shattered any remaining hopes with their grim announcement: Meng had been the victim of a "very serious crime." This revelation sent shockwaves through the community, turning grief into a quest for justice. The police, combing through evidence and analyzing mobile traffic data from the areas where Meng vanished and was ultimately found, were piecing together the puzzle of her tragic end.

The community's response to this tragedy was a poignant reflection of their collective sorrow. On 26 December, a sea of grieving individuals gathered at Korsør Station for a memorial service. Among them were several hundreds of mourners, including notable figures like Stén Knuth, the mayor of Slagelse Municipality, all united in their remembrance of Meng. This outpouring of grief was a testament to the impact of Meng's life and the depth of the community's loss.

As the year drew to a close, Meng's family made a heartrending request: the removal of all missing person posters. This act marked a painful acknowledgment of the closure of their search. Her funeral, held on 19 January 2017 in the historic St. Povl's Church in Korsør, saw her laid to rest in the Korsør Church cemetery, bringing a solemn end to her earthly journey.

The investigation continued with relentless determination. In June 2017, a significant development emerged when the South Zealand and Lolland-Falster Police released findings from their technical examination of a surveillance recording from Korsør Station. This footage, a crucial piece of the puzzle, showed an indoor corridor and a glimpse of the station's car park. Captured in this video was a faint image of a bright passenger car, roaming the area at about 4:07 a.m. on the fateful morning of Meng's disappearance. Despite the poor quality of the video, months of diligent work by experts abroad led to a hypothesis that the car was likely a Hyundai i30, model year 2011-2016. This clue was a beacon in the murky waters of the investigation.

The scope of the police effort was staggering: about 650 people interrogated, nearly 2,000 reports written, and approximately 400,000 cars compared with telephone information. Yet, the mystery of Meng's fate continued to haunt the community.

In a surprising turn in 2021, the case intersected with another high-profile crime. Danish police seized a white van once belonging to Peter Madsen, a convicted murderer known for the 2017 killing of Swedish journalist Kim Wall. They searched the van for possible traces of blood, a desperate attempt to link this vehicle to Meng's tragic end. However, this line of inquiry, like many before it, failed to provide the conclusive answers that Meng's family and the community so desperately sought.

The small, typically serene village of Kirkerup in Slagelse Municipality was thrust into a whirlwind of fear and uncertainty on the morning of 15 April 2023. It was a day that began like any other, but by 11:45 am local time, an alarming incident shattered the calm: a 13-year-old girl, known for her routine of delivering newspapers in the area, mysteriously disappeared. This unsettling news quickly rippled through the community, triggering a massive and immediate response from the authorities.

In a race against time, the police, collaborating with various agencies, deployed an extensive search operation. The skies above Kirkerup buzzed with the sound of drones and helicopters, while on the ground, search dogs scoured the area, all in a desperate bid to secure evidence and find the missing girl. The intensity of the search was palpable, with every resource being utilized in the hopes of a positive outcome.

As dawn broke the following morning, a local property became the center of attention, cordoned off by the police in a significant development in the case. Tension mounted as, at 10:57 am, the police authorities made a grave announcement: they were operating under the assumption that a crime had been committed. This statement marked a chilling turn in the search and heightened the urgency of the situation.

The event captured the nation's attention, drawing intensive media coverage towards Kirkerup, a village that until then had remained relatively obscure in the public eye. The story was not just a local affair but had become a national concern, with every development being followed closely.

In a dramatic turn of events, early in the afternoon, the police called for a press conference scheduled for 3:00 pm. The atmosphere was tense as the community and the nation waited for updates. However, moments before the conference was to begin, there was a breakthrough that would bring a mix of relief and shock.

Police inspector Kim Kliver, in a briefing that was briefly delayed, announced a significant development: a 32-year-old man had been arrested at his home in Svenstrup, Korsør. In a remarkable turn of events, the missing girl was found alive and conscious in his house, a discovery that brought an overwhelming sense of relief to a tense situation.

The girl's mother expressed her profound relief and joy, stating, "27 hours of nightmare is over and my dearly beloved Filippa is home." This sentiment was echoed by Danish Prime Minister Mette Frederiksen, who expressed her gratitude for the safe return of the young girl.

Norwegian NRK journalist Søren Arildsen captured the mood of the nation, describing it as a country that had been holding its breath for 27 harrowing hours, finally able to exhale. Almost all of Denmark, he noted, had become involved in the case, especially the local community, which had rallied together in concern and hope.

The investigation also saw the arrest of two other individuals, who were subsequently released the same day due to their proven innocence. By Sunday morning, the police had received an overwhelming 600 inquiries from locals, including crucial dashcam recordings, highlighting the community's deep engagement in the case.

Intriguingly, a connection to the murder of Meng, another high-profile case, was not publicly known at this point. It was only later, on 24 April, that the police confirmed a link between the two cases.

The unfolding drama of the case involving the 32-year-old defendant took a significant turn on 18 April, as the wheels of justice began to turn in earnest.

The stage was set at the Court of Næstved, where the defendant faced a crucial grundlovsforhør, a preliminary hearing in Danish law, charged with a litany of grave offenses. At precisely 11:46 am on 15 April, he was accused of initiating a prolonged deprivation of liberty, coupled with allegations of violence, threats of violence, and multiple counts of rape against the 13-year-old victim. The gravity of these charges cast a somber tone over the proceedings.

In a twist that added complexity to the case, the defendant entered a plea of "partly guilty." The court, weighing the severity of the charges and the evidence presented, ordered him to be pre-trial detained until 11 May. Adding to the atmosphere of intrigue, the judge issued an order prohibiting the public release of the defendant's name, a common practice in serious cases in Denmark to maintain the integrity of the judicial process. However, despite this ban, the defendant's name continued to circulate on social media, underscoring the intense public interest in the case.

The plot thickened on 24 April, when the B.T., a Danish newspaper, reported a crucial development: police had seized a white Hyundai i30 in Slovakia, a vehicle that the defendant had sold to a Slovak family back in 2016. This car was not just any vehicle; it was the same model sought by police in connection with the 2016 murder of Meng. This connection brought a new dimension to the investigation, linking the current case to a past unresolved tragedy.

Two days later, at a press conference held by the South Zealand and Lolland-Falster Police, another bombshell was dropped. The 32-year-old was now charged with Meng's murder and another unsolved crime that took place in Sorø in November 2022. This announcement sent ripples through the community, as it connected the defendant to a series of violent crimes spanning several years.

On the same day, the police revealed a startling piece of information: the defendant had been a person of interest in Meng's murder case back in 2016. He was among the 1,450 individuals from whom the police had collected DNA samples. However, the DNA sample collected from the victim at the time was too degraded and mixed to yield conclusive results with the methods available then, leaving the case unsolved until these recent developments.

As the case continued to unfold, the defendant, in a surprising move on 9 May, voluntarily prolonged his detention. This decision suggested a recognition of the seriousness of the charges he faced and the complexity of the legal battle ahead. The case, with its intertwining narratives and the specter of past unresolved crimes, continued to grip the nation, a grim reminder of the enduring quest for justice in the face of heinous crimes.

Seth Rich

Seth Rich's journey through life was a testament to his deep roots in his community and an unwavering commitment to political engagement. Born into a Jewish family in Omaha, Nebraska, Seth's early years were shaped by a strong sense of community and a keen interest in politics. His volunteer work with the Nebraska Democratic Party was an early indication of his passion for political activism. This enthusiasm was further cultivated through an internship with Senator Ben Nelson, providing Seth with a firsthand experience of the political process at a high level.

Beyond his political endeavors, Seth was actively involved in Jewish outreach, reflecting his dedication to his cultural heritage and the wider community. His role with the United States Census Bureau was another facet of his civic engagement, showcasing his belief in the importance of public service.

A pivotal moment in Seth's life came in 2011 when he graduated from Creighton University with a degree in political science. This academic achievement marked the beginning of a promising career in politics and led him to move to Washington, D.C. In the nation's capital, he joined the team at Greenberg Quinlan Rosner, a well-known polling firm, immersing himself in the world of political strategy and data analysis.

Seth's career trajectory took a significant turn in 2014 when he became a part of the Democratic National Committee (DNC). As the voter expansion data director, he played a crucial role in the party's efforts to widen its electoral base. One of his notable contributions was the development of a computer application designed to help voters find their polling stations, demonstrating his commitment to making the voting process more accessible.

However, Seth's promising career and life were tragically cut short. On the early morning of July 10, 2016, he was shot near his apartment in the Bloomingdale neighborhood of Washington, D.C. The events leading up to this moment were ordinary yet haunting in hindsight. Seth had spent the evening at Lou's City Bar, a local sports pub he frequented in Columbia Heights. After leaving the bar at closing time, he was unaware of the tragic fate that awaited him just a short distance from his home.

The police were alerted to the shooting by an automated gunfire detection system. Upon their arrival, they found Seth conscious but with multiple gunshot wounds. Despite being rushed to the hospital, he succumbed to his injuries, passing away over an hour and a half after the shooting.

The circumstances of Seth's death sparked widespread speculation and theories, particularly given the nature of his injuries and the fact that his personal belongings were not taken. His mother's emotional statement to NBC's Washington affiliate WRC-TV underscored the senselessness of the attack. She highlighted the physical struggle Seth endured and the puzzling fact that the assailants did not complete the robbery, leaving many to wonder about the true motive behind the shooting.

The investigation into Seth's death included a surveillance recording that offered a potential lead, showing the legs of two people who might have been connected to the crime. His family, friends, and the community were left to mourn a life that was not only full of promise but also deeply committed to making a difference. Seth Rich's untimely passing remains a poignant and unresolved chapter in the history of Washington, D.C., a reminder of the impact one individual can have and the profound loss felt when they are taken too soon.

The aftermath of Seth Rich's tragic shooting in July 2016 unfolded as a series of deeply emotional and complex events, resonating throughout his community and the political sphere. The day following the shooting, the Democratic National Committee (DNC) chair, Debbie Wasserman Schultz, issued a heartfelt statement mourning Seth's loss. She praised his dedication to voter rights, highlighting his significant contributions to the cause. This recognition from a prominent political figure underscored the impact of Seth's work and the depth of the loss felt by the DNC.

Two days after the shooting, the incident captured national attention when Hillary Clinton, a leading political figure, spoke about Seth's death during a speech. Her remarks were not only a tribute to Seth but also a call to action, advocating for the limitation of gun availability, thus bringing the issue of gun control into the national conversation in the context of this tragedy.

In the months following, Seth's family and his girlfriend appeared on the syndicated television show "Crime Watch Daily" in September 2016, discussing the murder case and keeping the public's attention on the unsolved crime. The following month, the DNC headquarters unveiled a poignant tribute to Seth: a plaque and a bike rack dedicated to his memory, serving as a lasting reminder of his life and dedication to the organization.

Further commemorating Seth's life, the Beth El Synagogue in his hometown of Omaha named an existing scholarship after him in February 2017. This scholarship, aimed at helping Jewish children attend summer camps, was a fitting tribute to Seth's commitment to his community and his Jewish heritage.

Amidst these memorials, the Rich family engaged the pro bono public relations services of Republican lobbyist Jack Burkman in September 2016. Burkman, alongside the Rich family, held a joint press conference on the murder in November of that year. In a bid to gather more information regarding Seth's untimely death, Burkman initiated an advertising campaign in Northwest D.C. in January 2017. This campaign included billboard advertisements and the distribution of flyers, reflecting the ongoing efforts to solve the mystery of Seth's death.

However, the investigation took an unexpected turn in late February when Burkman claimed to have a lead suggesting the Russian government's involvement in Rich's death. This controversial statement led to the Rich family distancing themselves from Burkman.

In a parallel development, the Rich family was approached by Ed Butowsky, a figure with connections to Fox News and Trump advisor Steve Bannon. Butowsky suggested that the family allow Fox News contributor and former homicide detective Rod Wheeler to investigate Seth's murder. The Rich family, seeking answers, permitted Wheeler to conduct his investigation. However, the family soon faced regret over this decision.

Wheeler's involvement in the case became controversial when he asserted a link between Seth and WikiLeaks in an interview with a Fox affiliate in May 2017, a claim he later retracted. The fallout from this interview led to the family's spokesman expressing regret over their collaboration with Wheeler. This incident culminated in Wheeler suing Fox News in August 2017 for mental anguish and emotional distress, alleging that he had been misquoted in a story that was published under the alleged urging of Trump.

Conspiracy Theories

In the wake of Seth Rich's untimely and tragic death, a whirlwind of politically charged and racially tinged conspiracy theories began to surface across various social media platforms. The very next day, the internet was awash with speculative narratives, as various groups started to weave intricate and often baseless tales linking his murder to a host of political intrigues. Among these, two theories gained particular notoriety: one alleging Rich's connection to the infamous 2016 DNC email leak, and another tying his death to the FBI's investigation into the Clinton Foundation. These claims, devoid of concrete evidence, nevertheless gained traction in the digital world.

The flames of conspiracy were further fanned by a Twitter post made shortly before Rich's memorial service, which insinuated that his death was not a random act of violence but a calculated political assassination. This notion quickly found fertile ground on the subreddit /r/The Donald, and before long, the website Heat Street had picked up the story, adding fuel to the speculative fire. Users on Reddit didn't stop there; they went on to associate Rich's murder with the long-standing and controversial 'Clinton body count' conspiracy theory. This theory then received a significant boost in visibility when Roger Stone, a political adviser to Donald Trump, echoed it on his own Twitter account, lending it a veneer of credibility in the eyes of some observers.

In a twist that added an international dimension to the saga, British journalist Duncan Campbell reported that the Russian intelligence agency, GRU, had made efforts to falsely implicate Rich as the source of the stolen DNC emails. This move was ostensibly an attempt to deflect attention from themselves, the true architects of the email theft. In a meticulous orchestration of deceit, the GRU allegedly altered timestamps on the DNC files to suggest that they were obtained just days before Rich's death. They even went so far as to adjust the time zone to Eastern Time, corresponding with Washington, D.C. In the guise of Guccifer 2.0, a supposed front for the GRU, they then fed the narrative that Rich had been their informant. This assertion, based on the manipulated data, led some experts to erroneously conclude that the emails were internally leaked from the DNC offices, rather than externally hacked.

In the intricate and often shadowy world of political leaks and cyber espionage, Julian Assange, the enigmatic founder of WikiLeaks, played a pivotal role in the saga surrounding Seth Rich's death and the DNC email leaks. His actions and statements, as detailed in various reports and interviews, added layers of complexity and intrigue to an already convoluted narrative.

On August 9, 2016, Assange appeared in an interview with Nieuwsuur, a

Dutch television program. The interview, intended to shed light on the risks faced by WikiLeaks' sources, took an unexpected turn when Assange, without prompting, mentioned the case of Seth Rich. This unsolicited reference instantly fueled widespread speculation about Rich's possible connection to WikiLeaks. When pressed to clarify if Rich was indeed a source, Assange maintained the organization's standard line of confidentiality, stating, "we don't comment on who our sources are". Despite this, WikiLeaks' subsequent communications stressed that they were not identifying Rich as a source, differentiating this case from their usual practice with other leaks.

The intrigue deepened with revelations from the Mueller Report. It outlined that WikiLeaks had received an email on July 14, containing an encrypted file named "wk dnc link I .txt.gpg" from the Guccifer 2.0 persona, identified as a front for Russia's GRU. This exchange occurred a mere four days after Seth Rich's tragic death. Adding another twist to the tale, Twitter direct messages unearthed in April 2018 suggested that Assange was actively seeking more emails from Guccifer 2.0, already suspected to be linked to Russian intelligence, even as he publicly hinted at Rich being a source. BuzzFeed, reporting on these messages, described them as "the starkest proof yet" of Assange's awareness of the true origins of the DNC leaks. They portrayed his actions as a deliberate attempt to mislead the public about the source of the leaked documents.

Mike Gottlieb, representing Rich's brother, pointed out the damning timeline: WikiLeaks received the stolen documents from Russian hackers four days after Rich was shot, a chronology that contradicted the narrative suggesting Rich's involvement. Julian Assange's role in this intricate web of deceit became even more apparent with the findings of Special Counsel Robert Mueller. According to Mueller's final report on Russia's involvement in the 2016 presidential election, Assange knew that the murdered DNC staffer wasn't his source. Yet, he continued to engage with his real sources within Russia's GRU, all while publicly insinuating that Rich was involved. This strategy, Mueller asserts, was an effort by Assange to obscure the true origin of the materials he was releasing.

The tangled web of conspiracy theories surrounding the murder of Seth Rich gained momentum and visibility through the active promotion by a cadre of high-profile individuals and media personalities. Among these proponents were Mike Cernovich, Sean Hannity, Geraldo Rivera, Kim Dotcom, Paul Joseph Watson, Newt Gingrich, Jack Posobiec, and Tim Pool. Their voices amplified these theories, injecting them into the public consciousness and lending them an air of credibility to certain audiences.

These conspiracy theories found fertile ground in the same digital and media ecosystems that had previously nurtured the infamous Pizzagate conspiracy. There was a striking similarity in the way both sets of theories were disseminated: each propagated by individuals and groups associated with far-right politics, and in some instances, by campaign officials and appointees in senior-level national security roles within the Trump administration. This crossover of promoters between the two conspiracy theories was not just coincidental but indicative of a broader pattern in the propagation of misinformation.

A key strategy in the spread of these theories was the use of social media, particularly Twitter and Facebook. Coordinated campaigns employed automated bots to amplify these narratives using branded hashtags, aiming to elevate them to trending topics and thus gain wider attention. This method was notably employed in both the Pizzagate and Seth Rich conspiracies, highlighting the sophisticated tactics used in modern misinformation campaigns.

The infamous subreddit forum /r/The_Donald played a significant role in propagating both theories, acting as a digital crucible where these ideas were forged and refined before spreading to a broader audience. A common tactic used by the promoters of these theories was to invert the burden of proof, challenging skeptics to disprove their baseless claims rather than providing substantial evidence to support them.

Commentators from various media outlets drew parallels between the two conspiracy theories, emphasizing their unfounded nature and the dangers they posed. Slate's Elliot Hannon likened the Seth Rich claims to the Pizzagate conspiracy, while The Huffington Post described it as a repeat of the 'alt-right' idiocy of Pizzagate. NPR's David Folkenflik and Margaret Sullivan of The Washington Post also drew similar parallels, underscoring the baseless and dangerous nature of these narratives.

Adding a further twist to the tale, a Yahoo! News article dated July 9, 2019, suggested that the origin of the Seth Rich conspiracy theory could be traced back to a bulletin purportedly issued by the Russian Foreign Intelligence Service on July 13, 2016. While The Washington Post's analysis questioned this conclusion, it acknowledged the significant role played by outlets like InfoWars, Fox News, and Sean Hannity in propagating these unfounded theories.

The web of conspiracy theories surrounding the tragic death of Seth Rich was met with a resolute response from law enforcement and reputable fact-checking organizations, all of whom unanimously dismissed these theories as unfounded and baseless. Despite this, the theories continued to circulate, highlighting a troubling aspect of misinformation in the digital age.

Law enforcement officials, including the Metropolitan Police Department of the District of Columbia, categorically stated that these conspiracy theories had no grounding in reality. They characterized Rich's murder as a tragic result of a bungled attempted robbery, firmly dismissing suggestions of any other nefarious motives or connections. Assistant Police Chief Peter Newsham specifically addressed the lack of any evidence linking Rich's death to the data obtained by WikiLeaks, reinforcing the police's stance that the murder was likely the outcome of a botched robbery.

Fact-checking websites such as PolitiFact.com, Snopes.com, and FactCheck.org conducted thorough investigations into these claims and reached the conclusion that the conspiracy theories were not only false but entirely without basis. These findings were a testament to the rigorous standards employed by these organizations in separating fact from fiction.

Colleagues and mentors of Seth Rich provided further insight, noting that Rich did not possess the necessary access or technical expertise to be involved in leaking DNC emails. Andrew Therriault, a data scientist who had worked with Rich, pointed out that despite Rich's recent work as a programmer, he lacked a formal background in programming. Another co-worker recalled Rich's distress upon learning about the DNC computer breach by hackers linked to Russian intelligence, indicating his disapproval of such actions.

Contrary to the false claims propagated by the conspiracy theories, the investigation into Rich's murder was led by the DC Metropolitan Police Department (MPD), not the FBI. This misinformation was another layer in the web of falsehoods surrounding the case.

High-profile individuals such as Newt Gingrich also played a role in promoting these baseless theories. Gingrich's claim of a link between Rich and WikiLeaks, suggesting an "assassination" tied to the leak of DNC emails, was completely unsupported by evidence and widely discredited.

Major news outlets like The New York Times and The Los Angeles Times described these conspiracy theories as "fake news," "falsehoods," and "unsubstantiated rumors," respectively. The New York Times highlighted the stubborn persistence of such fake news, coining the phrase "fake news dies hard." The Washington Post, in its analysis, showcased the virulent spread of fake news online, using the Seth Rich conspiracy as a case study. The Post noted that television news media was particularly susceptible to these false narratives. Additionally, the paper observed a decline in the spread of fake news on Facebook, but a continued prevalence on Twitter, often amplified by online bots.

The Washington Post's findings also revealed that the most potent conspiracy theories were those that appealed to both extreme ends of the political spectrum. The persistence of these false stories, even in the face of thorough debunking by fact-checkers, underscored the challenge in combating the spread of misinformation in the digital era.

On May 15, 2017, a pivotal moment occurred in the ongoing saga of the Seth Rich conspiracy theories, one that would further fan the flames of speculation and controversy. Fox 5 DC (WTTG), a local news station, aired a report featuring Rod Wheeler, a Fox News contributor and former homicide detective. Wheeler made explosive claims suggesting that Seth Rich had been in contact with WikiLeaks and implied a cover-up by law enforcement. These allegations, however, were not only uncorroborated but would later be largely retracted, casting serious doubts on their credibility.

The following day, Fox News, a national news outlet, escalated the situation by publishing a lead story on its website and dedicating extensive coverage on its cable news channel to what it described as Wheeler's uncorroborated claims about the Rich murder. In an unusual move, Fox News initially reported that Wheeler's claims had been "corroborated by a federal investigator who spoke to Fox News." This statement, however, was soon removed from their website as it became apparent that the claims lacked verification.

This reporting by Fox News reignited the conspiracy theories surrounding Seth Rich's killing. The impact of their coverage was immediate and significant, as evidenced by NPR's observation that Google searches for Seth Rich had surpassed those for James Comey, the former FBI director embroiled in his own controversy with President Trump, within a day of the original Fox report. The Washington Post's Callum Borchers pointed out the peculiar timing of Fox News' focus on the Rich story, occurring when most other media outlets were covering Trump's disclosure of classified information to Russia.

The narrative around Wheeler's involvement grew more complex as other news organizations began to delve into his background. It was revealed that Wheeler was not only a Donald Trump supporter but also a paid Fox News contributor. NBC News highlighted Wheeler's history of making sensational claims, including a bizarre assertion in 2007 about underground networks of violent lesbian gangs. The Washington Post underscored the unusual nature of Wheeler's relationship with Fox News, noting the rare circumstance of a news organization being so closely intertwined with the subjects of its coverage. Wheeler was simultaneously acting as a source for Fox, a paid contributor, and a purportedly independent investigator into the Rich case.

The complexity of Wheeler's roles and his appearance on Sean Hannity's Fox News show without proper disclosure of these multiple roles raised serious journalistic ethics questions. In the wake of Wheeler's Fox News interview on May 15, 2017, Brad Bauman, a communications professional representing the Rich family, expressed the family's distress. The Rich family requested that Fox News and its affiliate retract their reports and apologize, citing the damage done to their son's legacy.

The controversy surrounding the Seth Rich case was amplified by various claims and counterclaims, leading to a widespread dispute involving multiple parties. The family spokesperson, Washington, D.C. police department, the mayor's office of Washington, D.C., the FBI, and law enforcement sources knowledgeable about the case all contested the assertions made by Rod Wheeler, a Fox News contributor and former homicide detective.

The Rich family expressed their commitment to factual evidence and their frustration with the recurring emergence of unsubstantiated claims that they believed served only to distract from the real investigation into Seth's murder. Bauman, representing the Rich family, was particularly vocal in his criticism of Fox News. He accused the network of exploiting Seth Rich's memory for political purposes, specifically suggesting that their motivation was to divert attention from the Trump-Russia investigation.

In a notable development, Wheeler himself recanted his earlier claims in an interview with CNN, stating that he had no evidence to suggest Rich had been in contact with WikiLeaks. He also alleged that Fox News had misrepresented his statements, claiming that his information about the alleged evidence came from a Fox News reporter, not his own investigation.

Despite these clarifications, prominent Fox News programs, including Sean Hannity's show and Fox & Friends, continued to promote the conspiracy theory. Hannity's coverage included a segment with Jay Sekulow, where Rich's killing was framed as undermining the Russia investigation narrative. Notably, Sekulow had just been appointed as one of Trump's lead lawyers in the Mueller investigation.

The spread of the conspiracy theory was not limited to Hannity's show. Former House Speaker Newt Gingrich and Geraldo Rivera were among others who propagated these unfounded claims. Hannity also featured Tom Fitton of Judicial Watch, who discussed filing Freedom of Information Act requests related to the case.

Further fueling the controversy, Sean Hannity amplified baseless claims by Kim Dotcom, a New Zealand resident wanted by the U.S. on fraud charges, who alleged without evidence that he had been in contact with Rich before his death. However, Fox News host Julie Roginsky openly criticized the conspiracy theorists, condemning the exploitation of Rich's death and urging them to stop.

Criticism of Fox News's handling of the story extended beyond mainstream media, with conservative outlets such as the Weekly Standard, National Review, and columns by conservative writers like Jennifer Rubin, Michael Gerson, and John Podhoretz also voicing disapproval. In September 2017, NPR highlighted that Fox News had not issued an apology or provided an explanation for the discredited story.

By November 2020, it was noted that Malia Zimmermann, the Fox News reporter responsible for the retracted story, was no longer employed by the network. This sequence of events in the Seth Rich case reflects the complex interplay of media, politics, and public opinion.

On May 19, 2017, the ongoing controversy surrounding the murder of Seth Rich took a significant turn. The Rich family's attorney issued a cease and desist letter to Rod Wheeler, the private investigator whose claims had fueled the conspiracy theories linking Rich's death to the DNC hack.

Fox News, which had reported Wheeler's claims, retracted the story on May 23, 2017. The network removed the original article but notably did not issue an apology or explain the errors in their reporting. Despite the retraction, Sean Hannity, a prominent Fox News personality who had been a vocal proponent of the theory, remained defiant. He stated, "I retracted nothing" and vowed to continue seeking the truth. Fox News acknowledged that the original article had not undergone the rigorous editorial scrutiny typically required for their reporting.

On the same day as the retraction, Hannity announced on his show that he would stop discussing the issue, citing respect for the Rich family's wishes. Despite this, he maintained his commitment to pursuing the truth in future reporting. This decision led to a backlash from advertisers, with several including Crowne Plaza Hotels, Cars.com, Leesa Mattress, USAA, Peloton, and Casper Sleep withdrawing their marketing from his program. Some, like Crowne Plaza Hotels, clarified their advertising policies, and USAA eventually returned to advertising on Fox News after customer feedback.

The controversy deepened with the filing of a lawsuit by Rod Wheeler on August 1, 2017. Wheeler, who had initially claimed a link between Rich's murder and the DNC hack on Fox but later appeared to retract these claims, sued 21st Century Fox, the Fox News Channel, Fox News reporter Malia Zimmerman, and Ed Butowsky. He alleged that quotes attributed to him in the original Fox News piece were fabricated and included at the urging of the Trump White House.

The lawsuit included text messages and audio recordings as evidence. Notably, Wheeler and Butowsky had met with then-White House press secretary Sean Spicer to discuss the planned story. Texts from Butowsky to Wheeler suggested pressure from the highest levels, with mentions of the President's interest in the story. Butowsky also left a voicemail for Wheeler emphasizing the White House's attention to the matter.

Butowsky cited journalist Seymour Hersh in supporting the link between Rich and the FBI, a claim Hersh later called "gossip" and accused Butowsky of exaggerating. Butowsky also instructed Wheeler on the narrative to pursue in interviews, focusing on dismissing the Russian hacking story and its connection to the Trump campaign.

When the story aired on Fox News, it included quotes supposedly from Wheeler, framing the accusations against the DNC as coming from him. Wheeler contended that these quotes were fabricated and should not have been attributed to him. In subsequent recordings, Butowsky acknowledged to Wheeler that the claims attributed to him were false, yet hinted at some future recognition for Wheeler's supposed statements.

The lawsuit was dismissed in August 2018, with the judge ruling that there was no evidence of Fox manipulating Wheeler's statements on the recordings, and other statements were considered opinion. However, the discovery phase of this lawsuit provided information that the Rich family later used in their lawsuit against Fox News, which was initially dismissed but successfully appealed.

In May 2017, amidst the swirling conspiracy theories surrounding Seth Rich's death, his brother Aaron Rich issued a poignant statement. He expressed his family's desire to simply find Seth's killers and grieve in peace. However, they found themselves constantly battling against baseless allegations and misinformation to protect Seth's name and legacy. The family spokesperson condemned the ongoing conspiracy theories, attributing them to individuals with transparent political motives or sociopathic tendencies.

On May 23, 2017, Seth Rich's parents penned an emotional op-ed in The Washington Post titled "We're Seth Rich's parents. Stop politicizing our son's murder." In this piece, they appealed to the public and media to consider their feelings and cease using Seth's memory and legacy for political objectives. They expressed their anguish at the exploitation of their tragedy and urged those spreading falsehoods to allow them and law enforcement the space to find closure and justice for Seth's murder.

In March 2018, Aaron Rich took legal action against Ed Butowsky, Matt Couch, America First Media, and The Washington Times. He sued them for falsely suggesting he was involved in the alleged theft of emails from the DNC. In a significant development, The Washington Times retracted its related articles and issued an apology to Aaron Rich and his family as part of a settlement reached on October 1, 2018.

The Rich family also pursued legal action against Fox News. In March 2018, they filed a lawsuit against the network, reporter Malia Zimmerman, and contributor Ed Butowsky, alleging that a report published by Fox News fueled harmful conspiracy theories about Seth's death and caused them emotional distress. However, in August 2018, Judge George B. Daniels dismissed the lawsuit. He ruled that while the Rich family's belief that their son's death was being exploited for political purposes was reasonable, the plaintiffs failed to meet the stringent New York state law standards for "intentional infliction" of emotional distress.

The dismissal was overturned in September 2019 by the United States Court of Appeals for the Second Circuit, which found that the Riches had "plausibly alleged what amounted to a campaign of emotional torture." In subsequent proceedings, the Rich family utilized information from the unsuccessful Wheeler lawsuit to bolster their case against Fox News. This information highlighted Butowsky's involvement in the Fox News story, including his hiring of Wheeler and his meeting with then-White House press secretary Sean Spicer.

On October 12, 2020, Fox News reached a settlement with the Rich family. While the terms of the settlement were not publicly disclosed, it was reported to be a substantial seven-figure sum. The settlement also led to the dismissal of actions against Zimmerman and Butowsky, thereby eliminating the need for Fox News hosts like Hannity and Dobbs to testify. The agreement included a clause requiring the terms of the settlement to be kept confidential for a month. This series of events underscores the profound impact that media narratives can have on individuals and families, especially when personal tragedies are entangled with political agendas.

Sydney Land and Nehemiah Kauffman

The complex and often shadowy world of prostitution in the United States is exemplified by the intriguing situation in Nevada. Interestingly, in certain counties of Nevada, prostitution is legal, presenting a unique landscape in the American legal system. However, this legality does not extend to Clark County, the bustling home of Las Vegas, where prostitution remains illegal. This dichotomy creates a fascinating contrast within the state. Despite its illegal status in Las Vegas, it's estimated that the legal prostitution industry in Nevada generates a substantial $75 million annually. This figure pales in comparison to the staggering $5 billion estimated to be generated each year by illicit prostitution activities in Las Vegas, highlighting the vast and often hidden scale of this underground industry.

The issue of sex trafficking, a grave and illegal practice throughout the entire United States, casts a dark shadow over the world of prostitution. The complexities of this issue were starkly illustrated in a case involving Melanie Andress-Tobiasson, a Las Vegas judge, and her teenage daughter, Sarah. In 2015, Sarah, then 16, was employed at a local clothing store named Top Knotch. During her time there, Sarah observed activities that raised her suspicions of illegal sex trafficking occurring in and around the store. Alarmed, she reported her observations to her mother.

Andress-Tobiasson, deeply concerned for her daughter's safety and aware of the potential dangers of her being entangled in the world of sex trafficking, took decisive action. She reported the concerning activities at Top Knotch to the Las Vegas Metropolitan Police Department, commonly known as Metro, and specifically urged them to investigate the store owner, Shane "Suga" Valentine, whom she suspected of being involved in these illegal activities.

Expecting prompt and effective action from the authorities, Andress-Tobiasson was met with frustration when she saw no immediate response to her reports. This lack of action led her to suspect that Metro might be selectively enforcing the law, possibly collaborating with certain traffickers to target their rivals. Her concerns deepened when a meeting with Clark County Sheriff Joe Lombardo failed to yield any significant results.

Taking matters into her own hands in a bold and desperate move, Andress-Tobiasson personally confronted Valentine at his home. She intended to warn him away from her daughter and to express her serious concerns about his alleged involvement in sex trafficking. This daring act by a concerned mother and legal professional highlights the intricate and often perilous interplay between legal systems, individual actions, and the murky world of prostitution and sex trafficking in modern America.

In the sultry heat of August 2016, a young woman named Sydney Elysse Land, just 21 years old, embarked on a significant life change. Leaving the familiarity of her parents' home in Las Vegas, she ventured into independence by leasing an apartment at 4550 South Hualapai Way, nestled in the southwest part of the sprawling Las Vegas Valley. This move marked the beginning of a new chapter in her life, one filled with promise and the excitement of young adulthood.

Sydney's life, however, was intricately connected with two individuals who would play a pivotal role in the tragic events that unfolded. Her boyfriend, a former Centennial High School athlete named Nehemiah "Neo" Kauffman, aged 20, had a complicated background. Metro police had identified him as an alleged pimp, casting a shadow over his athletic achievements. Their association with two other figures, Frankie Zappia, a convicted prostitute, and

Dominique Thompson, Zappia's alleged pimp, further entwined their lives in a dangerous underworld.

The last time Sydney and Neo were seen alive was on the night of October 25, as reported by Zappia and Thompson. The following day, October 26, an unspeakable horror occurred. Unknown assailants brutally entered Sydney and Neo's apartment, a space that should have been a sanctuary of safety and love. The couple was mercilessly shot, each sustaining fatal head wounds in an act of cold-blooded violence.

The discovery of their bodies the next day, October 27, at 12:40 p.m., painted a harrowing scene. A neighbor, likely expecting an ordinary day, stumbled upon the grim reality: Neo's lifeless body sprawled on the living room floor and Sydney, tragically laid on the bedroom floor. This discovery sent shockwaves through their community and beyond.

Metro police, in the wake of the murders, faced a baffling case. They announced having no leads on a motive or suspects, deepening the mystery. However, they believed that two male perpetrators were involved, deducing this from the crime scene which showed no signs of forced entry, suggesting a disturbing level of premeditation or familiarity.

Steve Land, Sydney's grieving father, was fraught with not only the loss of his daughter but also frustrations with the investigation. Upon visiting the crime scene, he made alarming claims that the Metro police had left crucial evidence uncollected. Adding to his dismay, he revealed that neither he nor his wife, Connie, had been interviewed by the police in the aftermath of their daughter's murder. This lack of engagement extended to their home, where detectives did not visit to examine Sydney's room for potential clues.

This chilling case, marked by unanswered questions and a haunting lack of closure, encapsulates the dark underbelly of crime in Las Vegas. The tragic end of Sydney and Neo's lives, and the subsequent investigation, or lack thereof, reflect the complexities and often the inefficiencies within criminal investigations, leaving families and communities in a perpetual search for answers and justice.

The intricate web of events following the tragic deaths of Sydney Elysse Land and Nehemiah "Neo" Kauffman in Las Vegas unfolds like a gripping crime thriller, with twists and turns that captivate and perplex. At the heart of this mystery was Shane "Suga" Valentine, an associate of Kauffman, who quickly became a key figure in the investigation.

Valentine's entanglement in the case was rooted in a series of ominous events leading up to the murders. On October 8, a heated text exchange between Kauffman and Valentine escalated dramatically. Kauffman accused Valentine of being a police informant, triggering Valentine's ire. In a chilling turn, Valentine threatened not only Kauffman but also Land and her girlfriend, all while they were at a local Las Vegas casino. Later that day, Valentine's rage manifested physically when he rammed his rental car into the garage of Kauffman's mother's home and fired bullets into the residence, fortunately causing no injuries. Investigators recovered fragments from this alarming scene, including pieces of the car and a boulder used to smash a window.

After the fatal shooting of Land and Kauffman, a bullet from the earlier incident was discovered, intensifying the scrutiny on Valentine. The investigators pieced together that Valentine had fled to California in the same vehicle involved in the garage attack. Crucially, they retrieved the menacing text messages Valentine had sent to Kauffman, which contained explicit death threats.

Valentine's notoriety was compounded by accusations of attempting to recruit a judge's daughter into prostitution. He was arrested and arraigned for the firearms discharge on October 8, with his bail set at $50,000. In March 2017, he accepted a plea deal for these charges and was sent to Warm Springs Correctional Center. During his hearing, Connie Land, Sydney's mother, was present but not allowed to deliver a victim impact statement as the charges were unrelated to her daughter's murder. Kauffman's family was notably absent, and Valentine was never charged with the murders.

Despite initially being cleared by Metro as a person of interest, Valentine's involvement in the case remained a subject of renewed interest by October 2018. As of August 2019, he remained incarcerated, his connection to the murders still a topic of speculation.

Amidst this unfolding drama, Connie Land's pursuit of justice for her daughter was relentless. In early 2017, she reached out to the Investigation Discovery network and private investigators, desperate for answers. Her path crossed with Melanie Andress-Tobiasson, a Las Vegas judge, who shared Connie's concerns about sex trafficking in the city. Andress-Tobiasson believed Valentine was behind the murders and urged Connie to release confidential texts from a Metro homicide detective. Andress-Tobiasson even feared that she and her daughter were the intended targets of the killers, a theory that Connie found plausible.

Their alliance, however, was not without its challenges. The two women eventually had a falling-out. Andress-Tobiasson had been guiding Connie on which Metro detective to trust and claimed to have connections in the FBI. She promised that an FBI acquaintance would contact Connie, but this never materialized.

Frustrated with the perceived lack of progress from Metro, the Land family launched a high-profile campaign to keep the case in the public eye. They invested in digital billboards across key locations in Las Vegas, costing an astonishing $4,500 per day. Connie amplified this effort with frequent social media posts and appearances at press conferences, determined to keep her daughter's story alive and pressure the authorities for answers.

On April 12, 2018, the Las Vegas community was captivated by a compelling interview featuring Judge Melanie Andress-Tobiasson on KLAS-TV. During this interview, Andress-Tobiasson voiced a startling and controversial belief that sex traffickers in Las Vegas were specifically targeting the daughters of judges and law enforcement personnel, a claim that sent ripples through the community and law enforcement. Her assertion that the Metro police were not actively pursuing establishments acting as fronts for prostitution added to the growing tension. Andress-Tobiasson's admission that she feared the police more than the traffickers themselves painted a picture of deep distrust and concern within the legal and law enforcement communities.

In the wake of this interview, Metro officers began to submit complaints against Andress-Tobiasson to Sheriff Joe Lombardo. They accused her of committing ethics violations, particularly in relation to her personal involvement in the investigation of activities at Top Knotch, a local clothing store entangled in the case. Around the same time, the Nevada Current reported that Frankie Zappia and Dominique Thompson were named as suspects in the Land-Kauffman murders. By August 2019, Thompson was incarcerated on unrelated firearms charges, but no arrests had been made in the murder case, leaving a shroud of mystery and unresolved justice as of January 2023.

The aftermath of these events unfolded with increasing complexity and tragedy. In September 2020, Andress-Tobiasson found herself facing eight charges of judicial misconduct from the Nevada Commission on Judicial Discipline (NCJD). By May 2021, in a turn of events that shook the legal community, she resigned from her judgeship as part of a deal with prosecutors. This deal brought an end to the ongoing ethics inquiry related to her interest in the double-murder case. As a condition of this agreement, she vowed never to seek any judgeship, whether elected or appointed, in Las Vegas again.

Tragedy struck again in August 2022 with the heartbreaking news of Connie Land's death. This was followed by another shocking and sorrowful event on January 20, 2023. Andress-Tobiasson, who had recently been navigating the personal challenges of a divorce, was found dead from a gunshot wound in her Las Vegas home at the age of 55. In a turn of events laden with irony and sadness, the Clark County Coroner's Office ruled her death a suicide. This ruling was met with skepticism by some, including Dana Gentry, a Las Vegas blogger and acquaintance of Andress-Tobiasson. Gentry revealed to the New York Post a haunting statement from Andress-Tobiasson: "If I wind up dead, remember I wasn't suicidal." This revelation added a layer of mystery and speculation to her untimely death, leaving a lingering question mark over the series of tragic events that unfolded in the shadows of Las Vegas.

Abigail Williams and Liberty German

Liberty Rose Lynn German's story began on a winter's day, December 27, 2002, as she was welcomed into the world by her parents, Derrick German and Carrie Timmons. She was a cherished part of a large family, sharing her life with five sisters: Kelsi, Glenna, Alexis, and Hayden. A significant and profound relationship was formed with her grandparents, Mike and Betty Patty, who played an essential role in her upbringing, serving as her primary guardians.

From a young age, Liberty displayed an exuberant and creative spirit. She had a passion for baking, skillfully combining ingredients to create delicious treats, a reflection of her love for the culinary arts. Her artistic abilities extended to painting and crafting, where she expressed her joy and imagination through vibrant colors and diverse textures.

In her academic pursuits, Liberty was a standout. Her intelligence and drive for excellence shone brightly, pushing her to excel in her studies. She wasn't just a student aiming for good grades; she was determined to be the best in her class, embodying a competitive yet friendly spirit.

Liberty's energy and enthusiasm were not confined to academics. She was also an avid athlete, participating in various sports such as volleyball, softball, soccer, and swimming. Each activity showcased her commitment and spirited nature.

As an 8th grader at Delphi Community Middle School, Liberty celebrated her 14th birthday, a significant milestone that she shared closely with her best friend, Abby. Their friendship, which began in the 7th grade volleyball team, blossomed into an inseparable bond.

Abigail Joyce Williams, known as "Abby," was born on June 23, 2003, to Anna Williams. In the absence of her father, Abby's life was enriched by the love and support of her mother, her devoted grandparents Eric and Diane Erskin, and her extended family, including her aunts, uncles, cousins, and another grandfather, Cliff.

Abby had a free spirit and loved the outdoors, particularly enjoying ATV rides during camping trips with her family in Michigan. Her creative side was evident in her love for reading, photography, art, and drawing.

Initially reserved, Abby was known to open up and reveal a personality full of loyalty, love, and vivaciousness to those who became close to her. Hagen Jacobs, a family friend, highlighted her fearless and loving nature, noting her initial shyness but ultimate kindness.

Abby's talents were diverse, including playing the saxophone in the school band and participating in the volleyball team. As she approached her 14th birthday, she looked forward to high school and the new adventures it would bring, planning to face them alongside her best friend, Liberty. Together, they were poised to tackle the future, united by their strong bond and shared experiences.

On February 13th, 2017, a serene Monday cloaked in the anticipation of Valentine's Day, a unique occurrence unfolded. It was a planned snow day, a thoughtful provision in the school calendar to accommodate potential weather disruptions. Such days are earmarked at the start of the academic year, intended to prevent the school year from stretching too far into the summer months. Fortuitously, the winter had been mild, with no significant school closures, thus transforming this day into an unexpected holiday for students and faculty alike.

In the backdrop of this calm winter day, the lives of Abby and Libby, two inseparable friends, were interwoven ever more closely, not just with each other but with their families as well. The bond they shared was a testament to a year of growing friendship. The night before this unplanned day off, the girls had enjoyed a sleepover, reveling in the freedom and spontaneity that only teenage friendships can offer.

Embracing the unusually warm weather, a stark contrast to the typical winter chill, Abby and Libby impulsively decided to spend their day hiking. They chose a familiar spot, a trail known to Libby, aiming to seize the opportunity to bask in the outdoors.

Their adventure began around 1:45 PM, when Kelsi, Libby's older sister, kindly dropped them off at the trailhead. This trailhead, known as Freedom Bridge, is nestled along County Road West 300 North, adjacent to the Hoosier Heartland Highway. It lies in a wooded expanse a few miles from the heart of downtown Delphi, a setting that promised both tranquility and a touch of adventure.

The trail itself is a ribbon of history, following the course of an old, abandoned railroad track. It winds its way towards an iconic structure – the Monon High Bridge. Towering at approximately 60 feet, this bridge is the second highest in Indiana. Constructed in the 1890s, its age is evident in its structure, marked by numerous gaps that render a walk across it both exhilarating and cautious. Traversing this bridge is not just a physical act but an exercise in focus, as one must constantly be vigilant to avoid missteps over the creek far below.

Around half an hour into their journey, Abby and Libby shared their experience with the world through Snapchat. They posted a couple of pictures: a black-and-white image capturing the essence of the bridge and a poignant photo of Abby crossing it. These images, unbeknownst to anyone at the time, would soon gain significant attention, marking the girls' last known location.

An hour later, after these snapshots found their way to social media, Libby's father, Derrick, arrived for the pre-arranged pickup. Before reaching the spot, he attempted to call Libby, a routine check-in that went unanswered. Arriving at the location, Derrick was met with silence; the girls were nowhere to be seen.

Concern mounting, Derrick repeatedly called Libby's phone, each call echoing into the void of unanswered rings. He then embarked on a search along the trail, an effort marked by growing apprehension. During his search, he encountered an older gentleman, likely in his mid-to-late 70s, clad in a flannel shirt and also walking the trail. Derrick inquired about the girls, but the man hadn't seen them. It's important to note that this man, a mere passerby on the trail, is not considered to be involved in any wrongdoing.

As the afternoon waned, a small search party, consisting of Derrick and other family members, scoured the trail in search of Abby and Libby. But as the clock hands inched towards 5:30 PM, with no sign of the girls, the heavy decision was made to report them as missing. What started as a day of adventure and camaraderie had taken a somber turn, casting a shadow of concern over the Delphi community.

As dusk fell on February 13th, 2017, the urgency to find Abby and Libby intensified. After missing their designated pickup time, their family members started a meticulous search of the surrounding area. Realizing the gravity of the situation, at approximately 5:30 PM, the girls were officially declared missing to the Carroll County Sheriff's Department. This triggered an immediate and extensive search operation involving multiple agencies.

The search party was a collaboration of various local departments: the Carroll County Sheriff's Department, Delphi Police Department, Delphi Fire Department, and the Department of Natural Resources. Each team brought its unique expertise to the search, united in the singular goal of finding Abby and Libby. They scoured the area on foot, covering the rugged terrain near the Monon High Bridge – the girls' last known location as per the images posted on Snapchat. In a bid to pinpoint their whereabouts, efforts were made to ping the girls' cell phones. However, these attempts led to a dead end, suggesting that the phones were either out of battery or turned off, as they had ceased pinging earlier that day.

As the hours ticked by, the search continued under the cloak of nightfall. The challenging conditions – darkening skies and dropping temperatures – made the search increasingly difficult. The terrain around the bridge, already complex during daylight, became treacherous in the dark. The temperature, dipping below freezing, added to the urgency and complexity of the search. Despite the determined efforts of the search teams, the decision to halt the search was made shortly before midnight, as the conditions rendered further searching perilous.

At this juncture, law enforcement, led by Carroll County Sheriff Tobe Leazenby, did not immediately suspect foul play. The prevailing theory was that the girls were not in immediate danger from an external threat, but rather from the harsh environmental conditions. There was an underlying belief that the girls might have spontaneously decided to visit a friend's house, neglecting to inform their family – a hypothesis seemingly rooted in their young age and not much else.

This belief, however, would be tragically disproved in just over twelve hours. The initial assumption that the girls had taken an impromptu detour would soon be overshadowed by a grim reality, unraveling a narrative far more harrowing than anyone had anticipated. The hope that had flickered during those initial search hours would soon give way to a profound and unsettling truth, altering the course of the investigation and shaking the community to its core.

The dawn of Tuesday, February 14th, a day typically associated with love and joy due to Valentine's Day, brought with it a renewed sense of determination in the search for Abby and Libby. The quiet anticipation of the day was overshadowed by the urgency of the ongoing search.

As the morning sun rose, casting its light over Delphi, search crews reconvened near the Monon High Bridge around 10:00 AM. The plan was strategic and comprehensive – to fan out in different directions from the bridge and cover a vast expanse of the surrounding area in daylight. The search teams were not just on foot this time; they were augmented by K-9 units with their keen sense of smell and specialized dive teams prepared to scour the local water bodies. This multi-faceted approach underscored the seriousness of the situation and the commitment of the community to find the girls.

However, this day of searching would be markedly shorter than the previous one. A significant and heart-wrenching discovery was made by the Delphi Fire Department just after noon. Following a set of footprints, officials stumbled upon a scene about 50 feet from the north bank of Deer Creek, approximately half a mile east of the Monon High Bridge. The Delphi Fire Chief, upon discovering the scene, described it somberly as "not good." It was a grim revelation: the bodies of the missing girls had been found.

In the immediate aftermath of this discovery, details were scarce. Police, in an effort to maintain the integrity of the investigation and perhaps out of respect for the families, withheld most information from the public. The only piece of information that seeped through the tight-lipped response was the location of the discovery: a plot of land owned by a local resident, Ronald Logan. Authorities were quick to clarify that Mr. Logan was not involved in the crime; his land, a vast wooded area along Deer Creek, had simply become an inadvertent scene of a tragic discovery.

Later that afternoon, a press conference was convened, with representatives from the Delphi Police Department, Carroll County Sheriff's Department, and

Indiana State Police addressing the media. The atmosphere of this briefing was heavy with an unspoken sorrow, and the officials maintained a cautious approach in their communication. Details were kept to a bare minimum, and there was a noticeable reluctance to confirm explicitly that the discovery was indeed related to the missing girls. The community, which had been holding its breath in hope and anticipation, was now faced with a somber reality, enveloped in a shroud of mystery and unanswered questions.

On the somber day of February 15th, 2017, a chilling confirmation came from the police: the bodies discovered just a day earlier were, tragically, those of Liberty German and Abigail Williams. This heart-wrenching news followed closely on the heels of an autopsy conducted in Terra Haute, Indiana. The veil of mystery only thickened as the results of the autopsy were promptly sealed, shrouding the specifics of this tragedy, including the cause of death, in secrecy. Although the media had reported the girls' deaths as homicides, the authorities remained tight-lipped about the details.

In a significant turn of events, Sgt. Kim Riley from the Indiana State Police addressed the media with a determined statement that underscored the gravity and resolve of the investigation: a commitment to finding the perpetrator of this heinous crime.

As the investigation intensified, that very evening, the police released a photograph that would become central to the case. The image featured a man, previously unknown, who had been spotted on the same trail as the victims. Captured in a photograph that eerily showed him on the same bridge section featured in a Snapchat photo uploaded by the girls shortly before their untimely deaths, this man's image was a pivotal piece of evidence. Cropped from a larger picture, the image was frustratingly vague and heavily pixelated, making the man's features difficult to discern. Yet, from this elusive image, certain characteristics could be gleaned: the man appeared to be an average, possibly heavyset individual, clad in blue jeans, a navy blue jacket over a hoodie, and potentially sporting a paperboy-style hat. His posture, with head down and hands pocketed, added to the enigmatic nature of the photograph.

Initially, the police did not label this man as a suspect but rather as a person of interest whom they wished to interview. This status, however, shifted dramatically by February 19th, when he was officially declared the primary suspect in this harrowing investigation.

Amidst these developments, a remarkable act of bravery and presence of mind came to light. Liberty German, one of the young victims, had managed to capture not only this critical image of the man but also video and audio footage of him as he approached them. Her foresight to activate her phone's camera in such a perilous moment was nothing short of extraordinary. Liberty's actions, carried out in the face of unknown danger, provided the authorities with their first substantial lead in the case.

The retrieval of Liberty's phone, whether from the crime scene or through the cloud backup to which it was linked, remains unclear. Nevertheless, her quick thinking and courage in the face of fear have been hailed as instrumental in the investigation. Should this case ever reach a resolution, it will be in no small part due to the heroic and astute actions of 14-year-old Liberty German, who, in an unthinkable situation, may have helped to pave the way towards solving her own murder.

Liberty German's cell phone captured not just a fleeting image, but also audio and video of a man believed to be connected to the crime.

The footage, shrouded in secrecy and not released to the public, showed a man approaching the two girls, Liberty and Abigail Williams. The girls, with a sense of foreboding, had the presence of mind to record this encounter. From this video, a still image was extracted and circulated widely in the days following the tragic discovery of the girls. Although just a brief glimpse, it provided a crucial look at the man's appearance.

More haunting was the audio extracted from this video. The clip, chilling in its brevity, captured the man's voice instructing "down the hill." This phrase, it's widely speculated, directed the girls towards a particular area on the southeast side of the bridge, possibly leading them into a trap.

Liberty's bravery in recording this encounter suggests there was a longer video, possibly with the phone concealed to avoid detection. This extended footage, which the authorities have kept under wraps, might contain further insights into the events of that day. The decision to withhold these details is a strategic one, aiming to preserve the integrity of the ongoing investigation and any future legal proceedings.

As the case unfolded, the police released a profile of the suspected individual. He was described as a white male, with a height ranging between 5'6" and 5'10", and weighing approximately 180 to 220 pounds. His hair was noted as reddish-brown, but his age and eye color remained uncertain. Initially thought to be middle-aged, investigators later revised their estimate, suggesting he could be anywhere from 18 to 40 years old, with a possibly youthful appearance.

Dubbed "Bridge Guy" or "BG" in online discussions, this individual initially was just a person of interest. However, as the case progressed, his status shifted dramatically. The police soon labeled him a prime suspect in the murders, a turn of events underscored by statements from the Indiana State Police.

Several months after the incident, in June 2017, a composite sketch of this man was released to the public. This sketch, based on tips and follow-up investigations, was widely disseminated, becoming a key image in the ongoing quest for answers. Yet, as time passed, questions arose about the accuracy and efficacy of this sketch in aiding the investigation.

Spearheaded by a collaborative effort between the Indiana State Police and the Carroll County Sheriff's Department, the inquiry initially focused on the victims' inner circle. Family members, friends, and acquaintances were scrutinized, as is customary in the early stages of such investigations, to uncover any potential leads or connections that could shed light on the crime.

Parallel to these efforts, investigators broadened their scope to include registered sex offenders in the surrounding area. This approach, while not indicative of a sexual component to the crime, is a standard procedural step in investigations of this nature, aimed at exploring all possible angles.

Another key strategy employed by the police was the acquisition and analysis of security footage from nearby establishments. This footage was crucial in piecing together the movements of individuals in the vicinity of the crime scene on the fateful day. The investigators also delved into the world of digital forensics, scrutinizing cell phone records in an attempt to trace any devices that may have been in close proximity to Liberty and Abigail around the time of their deaths.

The thoroughness of the investigation extended to the virtual realm as well, with authorities meticulously examining the victims' digital footprints. Social media platforms such as Twitter and Facebook were combed for potential connections or clues that might point to the perpetrator or provide context to the events leading up to the tragedy.

This painstaking and expansive investigation drew national attention, catapulting the small town of Delphi into the national spotlight. High-profile figures like Nancy Grace, Dr. Oz, and Dr. Phil lent their voices and platforms to the case, each featuring it on their respective shows in 2017. This surge in media attention significantly increased public awareness of the case, far beyond the borders of Indiana.

In an unprecedented move, the FBI leveraged a network of approximately 6,000 electronic billboards across 46 states, disseminating images of Liberty and Abigail, as well as the suspect, in an effort to gather leads and information from the public.

The response from the public was overwhelming. By June 2017, a mere four months after the tragic event, the authorities had received an estimated 18,000 tips. This deluge of information necessitated the involvement of federal agencies like the FBI and Homeland Security, who provided logistical support in managing the influx. A specialized communications dish was set up to handle the high volume of calls, and many of these tips were channeled to FBI call centers for further processing.

However, with this heightened attention and influx of tips came a wave of challenges. The investigation was inundated with false confessions and a multitude of extraneous theories. Many individuals came forward claiming responsibility for the murders, yet lacked crucial details of the crime, thereby complicating the investigation.

On February 22nd, 2017, Indiana, police officials from various departments convened for a press conference that would resonate across the region and eventually, the nation. The atmosphere was palpable with emotion, as these seasoned law enforcement officers, with careers dedicated to public service and justice, grappled with their emotions while addressing the media and public about the case.

In this briefing, the police maintained a guarded stance regarding the specifics of the investigation. Details such as the exact manner in which Liberty German and Abigail Williams met their untimely demise, or how their bodies were discovered, remained undisclosed. The question of whether a murder weapon was being sought was also left unanswered. Even years later, these particulars continued to be closely held by the authorities, reflecting the sensitivity and complexity of the ongoing investigation.

Earlier, on February 16th, just two days post the discovery of the bodies, a significant development took place. The police executed a search warrant at a residence along West Bicycle Bridge Road, located about five miles from the crime scene and on the opposite side of Delphi. The residence was thoroughly examined for approximately two hours; evidence was collected, photographs were taken, but no arrests followed.

The investigation also cast its net over Ronald Logan, a resident of Delphi, on whose property the bodies of the girls were found. Logan, an older man with a history of minor legal infractions, primarily related to alcohol, was not known for any violent criminal behavior. He had been the owner of this property for over five decades and found himself under the microscope of the police in the ensuing weeks. Notably, on the day of the murder, Logan, despite having a suspended license, had driven to a dump to dispose of garbage. This coincidence did not escape the attention of the investigators, leading to a thorough search of his property the following month. Nevertheless, the police considered Logan's involvement as unlikely and eventually cleared him of any potential connection to the crime.

Logan later shared insights about his property, describing it as a rugged, heavily wooded area, frequented by hunters and fishermen. He emphasized the difficulty of navigating this terrain, especially with equipment, due to steep inclines and abrupt drop-offs. Reflecting on the distance between his property and the bridge where the girls were believed to have encountered their assailant, Logan expressed his belief in the implausibility of transporting the victims through such challenging terrain.

The police continued their meticulous search for clues within the specific timeframe of the crime, focusing on anyone who was near the Monon High Bridge between 2:30 and 5:30 PM on February 13th. They believed that anyone in the area at that time could hold vital information, whether as a suspect or a witness who might have crossed paths with the girls or the perpetrator.

Amidst the investigation, a peculiar account emerged, rooted in rumor yet intriguing enough to merit attention. Reportedly, a local woman encountered a young man near one of the Monon High Bridge trailheads, whose vehicle appeared to be broken down. The woman, sensing something amiss as the young man avoided eye contact and claimed he was awaiting his father's arrival, left the scene. Only after learning about the murders nearby did she report this strange encounter to the police.

Another point of interest in the case was a meat processing plant situated about 2.5 miles from the Monon High Bridge. This facility, a significant employer in the area, was known for its emotionally challenging work environment. The plant attracted a diverse workforce, some of whom had limited employment options and were not local to Delphi.

The connection between the plant and the case took a bizarre turn when, a week after the murders, a bomb threat was called into the facility. This led to a police raid where several items were seized, including a pair of boots. While the police officially stated that the bomb threat and raid were unrelated to the homicide investigation, this event fueled rampant speculation among locals and those following the case.

In response to this heinous crime, the community rallied together, demonstrating an extraordinary level of support for the bereaved families. This outpouring of compassion extended beyond emotional support, as residents and local businesses mobilized to aid the families financially during their time of profound loss.

Fundraising initiatives sprang up throughout the town, with local establishments dedicating proceeds and organizing events to assist with the costs associated with memorial services, funerals, and other expenses the families faced. One notable event was a motorcycle benefit held in February, which drew an impressive crowd of over 3,000 participants to Delphi, reflecting the strong community spirit and the collective desire to support the grieving families.

The reward fund, initially set at $41,000, witnessed a remarkable growth, swelling to over $200,000. This significant increase was bolstered by generous contributions from prominent figures such as Jim Irsay, owner of the Indianapolis Colts, and Pat McAfee, the team's former punter who had since turned entertainer. The fund also benefited from a plethora of fundraising efforts and crowdfunding campaigns initiated by the regional community, showcasing their unwavering commitment to aiding the investigation.

On February 18th, 2017, just days after the tragedy, a public memorial service was held at the school attended by Libby and Abby. The event was a poignant farewell, attended by thousands of people who came together to mourn and honor the memories of the two young girls. Earlier that day, a more intimate private ceremony was held, providing a space for the girls' friends and family to grieve privately.

The loss of Abigail and Liberty left an indelible mark on their loved ones. The girls had been integral to their families and, in a community as close-knit as Delphi, their absence was felt deeply. Their families found themselves in a relentless cycle of grief, constantly reminded of their loss by the presence of their daughters' images throughout the town.

The profound pain of this loss was articulated by Abby's grandmother, who likened the experience to enduring an open-heart surgery without anesthesia, a vivid metaphor for the enduring heartache that the families faced. This unimaginable loss left a void that seemed impossible to fill.

In the wake of the tragedy, the families initially maintained a low profile, allowing law enforcement to lead the investigation both publicly and behind the scenes. However, as the year progressed and with the case remaining unsolved, several family members came forward, seeking to reignite public interest and gather additional support for the investigation. They appeared on national television, sharing their heartbreak and appealing to the public for any information that could lead to a resolution.

Liberty's grandfather voiced a powerful message during one of these broadcasts, imploring anyone with information to come forward, emphasizing that in today's interconnected world, someone must know something. Similarly, Abigail's mother expressed a deep-seated fear that the mystery of her daughter's death could remain unsolved for years to come, a haunting prospect for any parent.

The FBI's involvement marked a significant escalation in the pursuit of justice, bringing a wealth of experience and resources to the table.

The FBI's early contributions to the investigation were pivotal. Their expertise in behavioral analysis offered a new dimension to the profiling of the suspect. The analysts from the FBI provided a nuanced understanding of how the perpetrator's behavior might have shifted in the wake of the crime, occurring on February 13th, 2017. They outlined several behavioral changes that might be indicative of the killer's response to their actions. These potential changes included altered sleep patterns, possibly as a result of heightened stress or guilt, and an increase in the abuse of drugs or alcohol, perhaps as a means to cope with the psychological aftermath of the crime.

Another critical aspect identified was a change in the killer's emotional state, such as heightened anxiousness or irritability, which could stem from the fear of being caught or the weight of their actions. The FBI also suggested that the perpetrator might exhibit an unusual interest in the case's media coverage, perhaps driven by a need to monitor the investigation's progress or out of a distorted sense of connection to the crime. Additionally, they highlighted the likelihood of the killer engaging in conversations about their whereabouts on the day of the crime, possibly in an attempt to establish an alibi or dispel any suspicions among acquaintances.

Greg Massa, acting as the FBI's Assistant Special Agent in Charge, played a critical role as the FBI's spokesperson in the early stages of the investigation. His presence at the press conference on February 22nd was notable, as he elaborated on the behavioral traits and actions the killer might have displayed post-crime. Massa's insights provided a framework for both the public and law enforcement to consider potential suspects, emphasizing behaviors that might betray a connection to the crime.

As the investigation continued to gain momentum, the involvement of agencies from Tennessee and Georgia illustrated the expanding scope and determination of the authorities to leave no stone unturned.

In the complex web of theories surrounding the murders of Abby and Libby in Delphi, one of the earliest and most intriguing propositions was the potential link to a similar, chilling case that occurred five years prior, about 400 miles away in Evansdale, Iowa.

On July 13th, 2012, a distressing incident unfolded in Evansdale. Two young cousins, 10-year-old Lyric Cook-Morrissey and 8-year-old Elizabeth Collins, vanished while on a bike ride in the downtown area. The discovery of their abandoned bikes in a nearby park sparked an extensive search operation. Tragically, the search culminated in the discovery of their bodies in a secluded, wooded area about 20 miles from their last known location. By this point, the investigation had turned cold, with no definitive suspects or persons of interest emerging despite extensive police efforts and media speculation.

The Delphi case, unfolding years later, bore unsettling resemblances to the Evansdale tragedy. Both cases involved the abduction of two young girls in broad daylight, with their bodies later found in rural, wooded areas. These eerie parallels extended to the circumstances of discovery - in the Evansdale case, hunters stumbled upon the remains. Furthermore, both cases were shrouded in mystery, with law enforcement withholding critical details such as the cause of death and the condition of the remains.

Delving deeper into the similarities, there were other uncanny coincidences. Both incidents occurred on the 13th of the month and unfolded during early afternoon hours. In both cases, the involvement of family members was quickly ruled out, suggesting the perpetrator was an outsider, likely unknown to the victims. This aspect is particularly striking, as most child abductions are typically carried out by family members or acquaintances, according to the FBI and the National Center for Missing and Exploited Children (NCMEC).

The rarity of such crimes is further underscored by FBI statistics. Between 1974 and 2012, only 15 instances of double abductions during daylight were recorded, highlighting the extraordinary nature of these crimes. The geographical proximity of the two cases, happening within a few hundred miles of each other, seemed to diminish the likelihood of them being coincidental, given the scarcity of such incidents.

Despite these compelling parallels, investigators overseeing both cases have publicly acknowledged that they have shared information and compared notes. Yet, they remain steadfast in their belief that the two cases are unrelated. This conclusion suggests that key differences exist between the two cases - differences that might include varying causes of death, unique DNA evidence, or other undisclosed factors.

In September 2017, more than half a year after the tragic deaths of Abby and Libby, Daniel J. Nations, a 31-year-old man, was arrested in Woodland Park, Colorado. Nations had been involved in an alarming incident where he threatened people with a hatchet on a hiking trail, coinciding with the time a bicyclist was fatally shot on the same trail. This arrest piqued the interest of investigators due to several factors linking Nations to Indiana, where the Delphi murders had taken place.

Nations was identified as a registered sex offender from Indiana, and at the time of his arrest, he was found driving with expired Indiana license plates. He had become homeless after leaving Greenwood, Indiana, in May 2017, a few months following the murders in Delphi. These circumstances led the police to consider him as a potential person of interest in the Delphi case.

Officials from El Paso County Sheriff's Department, who had arrested Nations in Colorado, noted "many similarities" between him and the unidentified suspect in the Delphi murders.

Daniel Nations had a troubled past, with several criminal acts to his name, including a 2016 incident involving indecent exposure and voyeurism in a women's restroom. His criminal history dated back to 2007 and included various offenses, ranging from drug-related charges to domestic violence. In 2016, he was convicted of domestic violence in Morgan County, Indiana. Nations' wife, Katelyn, later revealed to reporters that his issues with anger intensified after the loss of his brother to violent crime in January 2017, just a month before the Delphi murders.

Katelyn Nations acknowledged the resemblance between Daniel and the composite sketch released by the police in June 2017 but expressed doubts about his involvement in the Delphi case. She pointed out discrepancies, such as the distance between their residence and the crime scene, Daniel's lack of personal transportation, and differences in appearance from the figure captured on Libby's cell phone. Additionally, she noted discrepancies in clothing, specifically stating her husband did not own a jacket matching that of the suspect's.

After his arrest in Colorado for the hatchet incident, Nations, now 32, was sentenced to three years' probation. However, he remained in custody due to an outstanding warrant in Johnson County, Indiana, for failing to register as a sex offender. In January 2018, he was transferred to Indiana custody.

In February 2018, the investigators in the Delphi case announced that Daniel Nations was no longer an active person-of-interest. The reasons for this decision were not publicly disclosed, but several factors likely contributed to this conclusion. Reports suggested that Nations had a distinct limp and a smaller build than the Delphi suspect. His Southern accent differed from the voice in the audio recording released by the police. Additionally, there were indications that he might have had an alibi for the day of the murders and lacked the means to travel to and from the crime scene.

Despite the initial suspicion and the similarities that had drawn attention to Nations, he was ultimately not considered an active suspect in the Delphi murders. Nations reportedly provided his DNA to the investigators and expressed his frustration with being implicated in the case, emphasizing his desire for the truth to be known and to clear his name from the cloud of suspicion.

The arrest of John Miller in July 2018, more than a year after the tragic Delphi murders, sent ripples of intrigue and speculation through the communities involved in both cases. Miller, a 59-year-old resident of Fort Wayne, Indiana, located about 100 miles southwest of Delphi, was known among his neighbors for his reclusive and irascible nature. His demeanor and lifestyle painted the picture of a man who preferred to keep to himself, shrouded in his own world.

Miller's arrest, however, was not directly related to the Delphi case but was instead linked to a cold case that had haunted Indiana for three decades. This case was the horrific 1988 murder of April Tinsley, an 8-year-old girl whose disappearance and subsequent murder had remained unsolved. April had vanished while playing with friends, and the discovery of her body days later revealed the chilling reality of her fate – she had been strangled and sexually assaulted. The killer, in a brazen and haunting move, left behind taunting messages to the police and the family of young April, a sinister act that compounded the tragedy and left a lasting scar on the community.

The breakthrough in this long-standing case came with advancements in DNA technology, which enabled investigators to revisit the evidence and significantly narrow down the suspect pool. This investigative pivot eventually led them to John Miller, who had remained in the area all these years, lurking in the shadows of everyday life.

Upon his arrest, Miller not only confessed to the crime but later entered a guilty plea. His sentence: 80 years in prison, a term that virtually ensures he will spend the remainder of his life behind bars, paying for the heinous act he committed decades ago.

In the wake of Miller's arrest and subsequent conviction, the online community, particularly those following the Delphi case closely, began to draw parallels between him and the unsolved murders of Abby and Libby. The proximity of Miller's residence to Delphi, combined with his proven capacity for committing such atrocious acts, fueled theories and discussions among web-sleuths and case enthusiasts. Adding to this speculation was a haunting detail from 1988 – Miller had once taunted authorities with a message suggesting he might kill again, a detail that sent chills through those drawing connections between the two cases.

However, the link between Miller and the Delphi murders remains speculative, with law enforcement maintaining a cautious stance. Indiana State Police Sergeant Kim Riley, addressing inquiries about Miller's potential involvement in the Delphi case, commented that numerous names were being considered in the investigation.

On a fateful day in November 2018, in St. Louis, Missouri, a chilling crime unfolded. A man entered a Catholic Supply store and committed a heinous act. He sexually assaulted two women, and when a third resisted his demands, she was tragically shot and killed. This horrifying event not only shook the local community but also caught the attention of those following the Delphi case due to some striking similarities.

The description of the perpetrator in the St. Louis incident bore an uncanny resemblance to the man recorded on Libby German's phone in Delphi, Indiana, some 300 miles away. Witnesses described the St. Louis assailant as middle-aged, with a height between 5'7" and 5'9", and notably, he was wearing a paper-boy hat and a navy blue Carhartt-styled jacket. The parallels in the physical description and attire were eerily similar to the individual in the Delphi case.

Within days of the attack in St. Louis, police identified a suspect: 53-year-old Thomas Bruce. A former U.S. Navy veteran and once a pastor, Bruce had become an advocate for gun rights. His life, however, seemed to have taken a downturn. He and his wife had filed for bankruptcy in early 2017, and he was unemployed at the time of the attack in the Catholic Supply store. His physical resemblance to the Delphi murder suspect added another layer of intrigue to the case.

Bruce was swiftly arraigned on multiple charges, including first-degree murder, sodomy, armed criminal action, burglary, and tampering with evidence. On December 4th, 2018, he faced a staggering 17 felony counts. Further compounding his legal troubles, Bruce was also implicated in another crime in Jefferson County, Missouri. In this incident, he allegedly invaded the home of a 77-year-old woman, where he is accused of assaulting, sexually assaulting, and robbing her.

Despite these serious allegations and charges, it's crucial to remember that as of the recording of this episode, Bruce has not been convicted of any of these crimes. He has pleaded not guilty and awaits trial in custody. The legal principle of presumption of innocence remains a cornerstone of the justice system, and as such, Bruce's guilt has yet to be established.

The speculation connecting Bruce to the Delphi murders has been rampant online, but making such a connection is, at this stage, speculative at best. The legal proceedings against Bruce will undoubtedly be closely watched, and any developments or revelations that emerge could potentially shed new light on this complex web of cases.

The arrest of Charles Eldridge on January 8th, 2019, in Union City, Indiana, added another twist to the ongoing saga of the Delphi murder investigation.

Located approximately two hours southeast of Delphi, Union City became the focal point of intense public scrutiny following Eldridge's apprehension under disturbing circumstances.

At 46 years old, Eldridge found himself in a precarious legal situation after he was caught in a sting operation. He had purportedly arranged a meeting with someone he believed to be a teenage girl, who turned out to be an undercover police officer. Following his arrest, Eldridge reportedly made confessions regarding his involvement in inappropriate sexual conduct with a minor, separate from the incident that led to his arrest.

Eldridge's mugshot, once released, quickly caught the public's attention due to its striking similarity to the composite sketch disseminated by the Indiana State Police in the Delphi case. This resemblance sparked widespread speculation and discussion, with many people drawing parallels between Eldridge and the unidentified Delphi suspect.

In response to the growing public discourse and the visual similarities, Randolph County officials proactively shared information about Eldridge with the FBI, acknowledging the potential, albeit unconfirmed, link to the Delphi case. However, they were quick to temper the public's fervor with a word of caution. They stressed that, aside from a superficial resemblance to the sketch, there was no concrete evidence connecting Eldridge to the Delphi murders. The cautionary message from the officials aimed to temper the public's tendency to leap to conclusions based solely on appearances, highlighting the potential harm such speculation could cause to an ongoing investigation.

Despite Eldridge's unnerving online behavior and his physical resemblance to the suspect sketch, there remained a lack of tangible evidence linking him to the tragic fate of Abigail Williams and Liberty German. As he awaited trial on the charges of child molestation, the case against him in relation to the Delphi murders remained unsubstantiated.

In an effort to manage public speculation and assure the community that progress was being made, Captain Dave Bursten of the Indiana State Police addressed the public directly. He emphasized the commitment of the law enforcement agencies to the case and reassured the community that any significant developments, including the arrest of a suspect in the Delphi murders, would be promptly and transparently communicated.

On the 22nd of April in the year 2019, an air of anticipation and uncertainty enveloped the community as the investigators of the Delphi double-murder case made a striking announcement. This date, etched in the memories of those following the case, marked a pivotal shift in the investigation's trajectory. Only a handful of days earlier, an intriguing hint was dropped by the authorities about a "new direction" for the case, setting the stage for a highly anticipated press conference.

This conference was not just another routine update. It was a moment filled with emotions and unanswered questions for the families of Abby and Libby, the young victims at the heart of this mystery. These families, who were about to be ushered into a world of new information, had a private meeting with the police shortly before the public revelation on that fateful Monday.

The press conference, orchestrated by Indiana State Police Superintendent Doug Carter, was a significant event. Superintendent Carter had become a familiar face in the case, having been deeply involved for over two years. The setting for this crucial update was the Canal Center in Delphi, Indiana, where an eclectic crowd gathered. This assembly included grieving family members, inquisitive reporters, and curious members of the public. There was even speculation that among the audience might be the very perpetrator of the crime, a chilling thought that added a layer of intensity to the event.

During this conference, Superintendent Carter delivered revelations that fundamentally altered the course of the investigation. The information previously disclosed by the authorities was now being revised, a clear sign that the case was entering uncharted territory. The most striking update was the release of a new composite sketch, a stark contrast to the one released back in June 2017.

This new sketch depicted a markedly different individual - younger, with distinctive features like a narrow nose, thin lips, and a pronounced jawline that could indicate an under-bite. The sketch also portrayed the individual with thick, possibly curly hair, and devoid of any facial hair. It represented a significant departure from the older image, now showing someone who could easily blend into the thousands of young men in the region.

The artist behind this pivotal sketch, ISP Master Trooper Taylor Bryant, emphasized that it was based solely on an eyewitness's account, untainted by other authorities' inputs or extraneous information. Intriguingly, this sketch was created shortly after the tragic discovery of the girls' bodies, on February 17th, 2017, yet it was held back from the public eye until this moment.

Meanwhile, the original composite sketch, as stated by Indiana State Police Sergeant Kim Riley, had lost its relevance in the ongoing investigation. It no longer represented a person of interest, suggesting that the individual depicted had been identified and absolved of any connection to the crime.

Accompanying the release of this new sketch was a significant update regarding the suspected age of the perpetrator. The previous belief that the killer was middle-aged was now replaced with a broader age range, anywhere between 18 and 40 years old. This wide spectrum acknowledged the possibility that the killer might appear deceptively younger than his actual age.

For the first time, police publicly theorized that the killer was likely not an outsider to Delphi. This new perspective suggested that the perpetrator was someone with a connection to the area – perhaps a resident, a worker, or someone with other reasons to frequent Delphi.

In a move that provided a new dimension to the case, police released a video fragment showing the unknown individual walking on the High Bridge. The footage revealed an unusual gait, possibly influenced by the challenging structure of the bridge, characterized by significant gaps between its ties.

The intricate tapestry of the Delphi murder investigation was further enriched with the introduction of a new, yet mysterious element - a car, observed in a location proximate to the crime scene, igniting a fresh wave of curiosity and speculation. This vehicle, which had been parked along County Road 300 North near the trailhead leading to the bridge, close to the Hoosier Heartland Highway, became a focal point of interest. It was noted to have been there during a critical time window on Monday, February 13th, 2017, between 12:00 PM and 5:00 PM. This seemingly innocuous detail transformed into a significant clue, as the car was positioned outside an abandoned CPS/DCS/Welfare building, a structure that has since been razed, leaving behind only the echoes of its past.

In a move that both intrigued and frustrated the public, the authorities kept the specifics of the vehicle - its make, model, or color - shrouded in secrecy. Their intention was clear: they sought to sift through potential leads with precision, filtering credible information from those who might genuinely recognize the vehicle, thereby narrowing their search for its owner.

This development dovetailed with local whispers of a woman's encounter with a young man in a truck near the scene, fueling theories that this new lead could pivot the investigation in an unexpected direction. The ambiguity surrounding the vehicle played into a larger narrative of uncertainty and hope in the relentless pursuit of justice.

Superintendent Doug Carter of the Indiana State Police, in a pointed written statement directed at the unknown perpetrator, left no doubt about the determination of the investigators. His words were a blend of warning and resolve, hinting at the mistakes made by the killer and the relentless pursuit that lay ahead.

The ongoing collaboration in this case is a testament to its complexity and the commitment to finding answers. Beyond the Indiana State Police, this collaborative effort spans the FBI, Carroll County Sheriff's Office, and even reaches into other states. In 2018, the Georgia Bureau of Investigation, along with other FBI field offices, was brought in to provide fresh perspectives. This cross-state cooperation, buoyed by federal involvement, has fostered a renewed hope that the perpetrator's capture is drawing near.

Meanwhile, the community, still reeling from the loss of Abigail Williams and Liberty German, has rallied in an extraordinary display of solidarity and remembrance. An initiative launched in 2017, involving the installation of orange light bulbs across Indiana, serves as a dual symbol - a tribute to the lost girls and a somber reminder that their killer remains at large. This communal act of defiance and mourning underscores the collective unease and determination that pervades the state.

As the two-year anniversary of the tragic incident passed, a renewed wave of optimism surged through the community and the families of the victims. There's a palpable sense that the extensive public knowledge about the case will eventually lead to the crucial tip that brings the perpetrator to justice. The hope is that the steady stream of information reaching law enforcement will eventually include the key piece of evidence needed to solve this heinous crime.

Mike Patty, Liberty German's grandfather, in a heartfelt appeal to the Lafayette Journal & Courier, underscored the belief that the community holds the key. His conviction that someone out there holds a crucial piece of information, however insignificant it might seem, could be the linchpin in resolving this mystery.

As the investigation marches on, the public remains largely in the dark about the finer details of the case. The police, in their strategic discretion, have kept most of their evidence confidential, including the status of any DNA evidence they might possess. It's widely speculated that they have a DNA sample, possibly partial, which could be instrumental in eliminating suspects but not comprehensive enough for identification through DNA databases. This painstaking process of elimination, involving DNA submissions from various suspects and persons of interest, highlights the meticulous and thorough nature of the investigation.

In summary, the Delphi murder case, with its complex web of clues, theories, and unyielding search for truth, continues to captivate and haunt those touched by the tragedy. The determination of the investigators, the resilience of the community, and the enduring hope for justice form the cornerstone of this ongoing quest to bring closure to a case that has deeply affected so many lives.

Barry and Honey Sherman

Bernard Charles "Barry" Sherman's story is a fascinating journey of intellectual brilliance and business acumen, beginning in the bustling city of Toronto, Ontario. Born on February 25, 1942, Sherman quickly distinguished himself as a prodigious talent. His early life in Toronto set the stage for an illustrious academic and professional career. He attended the prestigious Forest Hill Collegiate Institute, where he was not just a student but a shining example of academic excellence, graduating with high marks that were a testament to his diligence and intelligence.

Sherman's academic journey took a remarkable turn when, at the tender age of 16, he became one of the youngest students ever to enroll in the University of Toronto's esteemed Engineering Science program. This achievement was not just a reflection of his intellectual capabilities but also a clear indicator of his relentless pursuit of knowledge and excellence.

In 1964, Sherman's hard work and dedication culminated in his graduation with top honors, a significant milestone that was further embellished with a university award for his exceptional thesis. However, his thirst for knowledge was far from quenched. Sherman embarked on another academic adventure, this time delving into the complex world of astrophysics. His journey led him to the renowned Massachusetts Institute of Technology, where in 1967, he earned a Ph.D., adding another feather to his already impressive academic cap.

But Sherman's story was not just one of academic triumphs. After obtaining his Ph.D., he ventured into the pharmaceutical industry, marking the beginning of a new chapter in his life. Along with his business partner Joel Uster, Sherman made a strategic move by purchasing Empire Laboratories. This acquisition was not just a business transaction but a pivotal moment in his career, as the company was previously owned by his uncle, Louis Lloyd Winter, who had passed away in 1965.

The acquisition of Empire Laboratories was a complex affair, involving an intricate deal with Winter's four sons – Paul, Jeffrey, Kerry, and Dana – who were also Sherman's cousins. In a move that demonstrated Sherman's business savvy and foresight, the deal included offering equity and royalties on several of Empire's patented products to Winter's sons.

This critical decision, made in the early stages of his business career, had far-reaching implications. The deal, often scrutinized and debated by case observers, was not just a business arrangement but a family affair that intertwined personal relationships with professional dealings. Tragically, this deal would later be speculated as a potential motive in the untimely and mysterious deaths of Barry and his wife, Honey Sherman, weaving a complex tapestry of success, family ties, and unsolved mystery.

The tale of Barry and Honey Sherman is one of love, family, entrepreneurial spirit, and profound impact on both the pharmaceutical industry and philanthropic endeavors. In 1971, Barry Sherman, a figure already making waves in the pharmaceutical world, married Anna Debra "Honey" Reich. Honey, born on January 25, 1947, in Austria, brought a vibrant and complementary presence to Barry's life. The couple, over the span of about 16 years from around 1974 to 1990, welcomed four children into their lives: Lauren, Jonathon, Alexandra, and Kaelen. The Shermans' household was a blend of warmth, unity, and the hustle of a growing family. To the outside world, their marriage was the epitome of happiness, a perfect blend of love and mutual respect, forming a close-knit family unit that was the envy of many.

Barry, known for his intense focus and dedication to his work, often appeared as a standoffish workaholic. He was not one to eagerly partake in family vacations or social gatherings, his mind often preoccupied with the intricacies of his business ventures. In contrast, Honey was the social heartbeat of the family. Known for her affable and outgoing personality, she was not just the glue that held the family together but also a passionate philanthropist, deeply involved in various charitable causes and community work, embodying the spirit of generosity and kindness.

In the business world, 1972 marked a pivotal year for Barry Sherman. He and his partner decided to sell Empire Laboratories, paving the way for what would become his most significant business venture. Soon after, Sherman founded Apotex in 1974, a company that would grow to become a juggernaut in the production of generic drugs. The initial years were a struggle, a testament to Sherman's perseverance and business acumen. However, his relentless pursuit of excellence and strategic business moves paid off as Apotex witnessed exponential growth throughout the 1980s and '90s. The company became a household name in the pharmaceutical industry, known for its popular generic versions of prescription drugs and a series of strategic acquisitions of other pharmaceutical companies.

By 2023, the impact of Sherman's vision and entrepreneurial skills was evident. Apotex's annual sales soared beyond $2.5 billion, a staggering figure that reflected the company's dominance in the market. Barry Sherman's personal wealth, a direct result of his unwavering dedication and business prowess, was estimated to be at least $3.2 billion. This astounding figure placed him among the top 15 richest individuals in Canada at the time of his death.

Barry Sherman's journey with Apotex was not only marked by tremendous success in the pharmaceutical industry but also by a series of intriguing forays into various other business ventures. These ventures, often diverging significantly from his primary pharmaceutical interests, paint a picture of a man whose business acumen was matched by a certain audacity to explore the unknown and, at times, the unconventional.

Sherman's choices in these ventures often raised eyebrows, oscillating between what appeared to be naivety and dealings that seemed to tread the line of being somewhat dubious. It was as if Sherman, bolstered by his substantial financial success, was driven by a blend of generosity and a sense of adventure in his investments, even if they seemed foolhardy to the more cautious observer. This trait, perhaps stemming from his ability to afford such risks, led to a number of notable, if not always successful, investments outside of his pharmaceutical empire.

Colleagues and business associates observed Sherman's approach with a mix of admiration and concern. One Apotex employee reflected on this aspect of Sherman's character, suggesting that his generosity and trusting nature might have made him vulnerable to exploitation, particularly in his less familiar business ventures. A business associate echoed this sentiment, noting that Sherman often financed projects with little hope of success, driven perhaps by his desire to support the underdog or a belief in the potential of the unlikely.

One of Sherman's more infamous investments was in a yacht company that turned out to be a façade for an illegal tax shelter. This venture culminated in one of the largest tax frauds in Canadian history when it was revealed that the yachts, the supposed heart of the business, were non-existent. Sherman's response to this fiasco was to sue his accountants for negligence after losing $600,000. However, the Ontario Court of Appeal, in a ruling covered by Canadian magazine Maclean's, opined that Sherman, an 'astute businessman' and 'experienced investor,' should have been more vigilant, essentially stating that he should have known better.

Sherman's ventures sometimes led him into the company of controversial figures. In the 1990s, he bought a stake in a nutritional supplement company started by Kevin Trudeau, an American fraudster known for his infomercial pitches and criminal scams, who was eventually fined and imprisoned.

Sherman's involvement in this venture was a testament to his willingness to take risks, even in the face of potential controversy.

Another notable association was with Frank D'Angelo, a controversial entrepreneur known for a series of ambitious but ultimately unsuccessful ventures. Sherman's investment in D'Angelo's endeavors, which included a brewery, films, energy drinks, and other businesses, was substantial. The bankruptcy of "D'Angelo Brands" in 2007 resulted in Sherman losing a staggering $100 million, a testament to the risks inherent in his investment strategy.

In 2015, Sherman's penchant for high-risk investments led him to Shaun Rootenburg, an American ex-convict and con artist. Sherman was persuaded to invest in an online video game app, a venture that promised much but ultimately resulted in another loss, as the app never materialized.

In the fiercely competitive world of generic drug manufacturing, the path to success often requires a degree of ruthlessness, and Barry Sherman, at the helm of Apotex, was a textbook example of this. His tenure at Apotex was marked by a relentless pursuit of dominance in the industry, a journey that wasn't without its share of controversy and aggressive strategies.

Sherman was often embroiled in practices that drew criticism and legal scrutiny. He faced allegations ranging from engaging in price-fixing to the utilization of fraudulent data. His business dealings occasionally veered into murky waters, involving interactions with individuals of dubious repute. Additionally, his approach to policy influence raised ethical questions, and he was implicated in a medical research scandal that had dire consequences for a doctor's career and reputation.

Known for his litigious nature, Sherman was not one to shy away from legal confrontations. His strategy often involved deploying a barrage of lawsuits against competitors, regulatory bodies in Canada, and essentially any entity that he perceived as a threat or obstacle. This propensity for legal warfare was indicative of his aggressive approach to business and his unyielding determination to protect and advance his interests.

Barry's son, Jonathon Sherman, offered a candid portrayal of his parents to the police. He described his father as "brilliant but lacking in emotional and social intelligence," painting a picture of a man whose intellectual prowess was not mirrored in his emotional and social dealings. On the other hand, he characterized his mother, Honey, as "smart, abrasive, high-energy," suggesting a complex personality that was both formidable and dynamic.

Honey Sherman, while widely respected for her prowess as a fundraiser, had interactions with others that were often remembered with a mix of admiration and criticism. She was described by some as "loud and obnoxious" and "difficult," and there were reports of her being demanding and entitled in her dealings. These descriptions depict a woman of strong character and presence, unafraid to assert herself but also capable of ruffling feathers.

The use of charitable foundations by the Shermans also came under scrutiny. Allegations surfaced that Barry Sherman was utilizing these foundations to receive tax credits while effectively loaning the money back to himself. This maneuver, described by one watchdog group as "using his foundations as a piggy bank," highlighted a savvy, if controversial, exploitation of the system. While this practice was not illegal, it certainly raised ethical questions and cast a shadow over the couple's philanthropic efforts. It remained unclear whether Honey was aware of these financial strategies. Regardless, this aspect of their charitable work, rightly or wrongly, tarnished the public perception of their otherwise commendable philanthropic contributions, adding yet another layer of complexity to the Shermans' multifaceted public personas.

Barry Sherman's life, marked by remarkable business acumen and legal battles, featured a particularly contentious and prolonged legal dispute with his four cousins, the Winter brothers. This dispute was deeply rooted in a family business saga that began with the death of their father, Louis Lloyd Winter, when the brothers were all children under the age of seven.

After Louis Lloyd Winter's passing, Sherman took over the reins of Empire Laboratories, the family business. However, this transition was not without its controversies. Years later, the Winter brothers brought a lawsuit against Sherman. Their claim was steeped in a sense of betrayal and loss; they alleged that Sherman had unjustly sold their father's company, effectively denying them their rightful opportunity to stake a claim in Empire Laboratories. This accusation hinged on a protection clause in the original contract, which, according to the brothers, should have allowed them the first right to make an offer on Empire before its sale.

The legal battle that ensued was intense and emotionally charged. The courts, however, found no merit in the Winter brothers' claims. In a decision that might have seemed like a vindication for Sherman, the court labeled the brothers' interpretation of the contract as "wishful thinking." In a further twist, the court ordered the Winter brothers to pay Sherman's attorney fees, amounting to around $300,000, a ruling that only added fuel to the already blazing familial discord.

To describe the resulting animosity within the family as mere "bad blood" would be a gross understatement. Particularly aggrieved was Kerry Winter, who did not mince words in expressing his deep-seated anger towards his cousin in various interviews. His vocal outrage was a stark manifestation of the bitterness and resentment that this legal feud had sowed within the family.

The fallout from this familial and legal strife contributed to a growing list of individuals who, in the eyes of some, might have harbored motives for harboring ill will against Barry Sherman. This list, as it turned out, was not short. It included a range of characters, each with their own grievances, be they real or perceived, against the pharmaceutical magnate.

The morning of December 15, 2017, unfolded with a scene straight out of a mystery novel at the Sherman mansion, a grandiose residence that had recently been listed on the market. Real estate agents, eager to showcase this prime property, escorted a couple, potential buyers, through the elegant expanse of the main house. The tour, up to that point, was routine and uneventful. However, as the group descended to the basement to view the luxurious amenities of a hot tub and lap pool, they stumbled upon a scene that was shockingly out of place in the opulent setting.

There, in a chilling and macabre tableau, lay the bodies of Barry and Honey Sherman. The couple was found side by side, their necks grotesquely tied to a metal railing encircling the pool. The scene was one of stark horror and disbelief. Investigators later deduced that the Shermans had likely met their tragic end approximately 36 hours earlier, on December 13th. At the time of their deaths, Barry was 75 and Honey was 70, their lives ending in a manner as mysterious as it was tragic.

The immediate aftermath of this grisly discovery was fraught with confusion and speculation. The post-mortem investigation revealed that both Barry and Honey had died from "ligature neck compression." The absence of forced entry and any signs of a robbery led the police to initially steer away from suspecting an external perpetrator. This stance by the authorities fueled rampant speculation, with theories ranging from a murder-suicide to a suicide pact between the couple. One officer even ventured to dismiss the possibility of a double homicide, a conclusion that only deepened the mystery surrounding the deaths.

The Sherman children, in response to the swirling theories, issued a vehement statement rejecting the notion of their parents' suicide. They pointed to several compelling aspects of Barry and Honey's lives that contradicted such a theory: the couple's active involvement in designing a new home, upcoming holiday plans in Miami, planned trips to Japan and Israel, and the recent joy of a new grandchild. The idea that Barry would take his own life and that of his wife was unthinkable to those who knew them.

Moreover, the physical evidence at the scene raised serious doubts about the suicide hypothesis. Questions emerged about the feasibility of a 75-year-old Barry Sherman managing to transport Honey's body to the basement pool area, let alone orchestrating the grim scene of their hanging. What possible motive could there be? Additionally, marks on their wrists suggested the use of zip ties, an element seemingly incongruent with a murder-suicide scenario.

Observers also questioned the likelihood of a pharmaceutical mogul, with easy access to more direct and less painful methods, choosing such a convoluted method for suicide. It seemed implausible that Sherman, with his extensive knowledge of pharmaceuticals, would opt for such a complex and physically demanding method of ending his life.

The perplexing case of the Shermans' untimely demise continued to baffle investigators as they delved deeper into the circumstances surrounding their deaths. One particularly puzzling aspect was the positioning of their bodies, which appeared almost theatrical in nature, as if deliberately posed or staged, adding a layer of eerie premeditation to the scene.

This notion of staging was further fueled by a rather eerie observation made by some who were familiar with the Sherman household. In the Shermans' recreation room, there was a distinctive "junk sculpture" art piece, a creative assembly of male and female figures crafted from discarded materials. These figures were designed to be seated with their legs crossed, presenting a striking and somewhat haunting image. While there wasn't a direct replication of this sculpture in the way the Shermans were found, the similarities were uncanny enough to lead to speculation that the positioning of their bodies might have been a deliberate attempt to mirror this artwork. This theory, while speculative, lent a more sinister and personal angle to the crime, suggesting a level of thought and intention that went beyond a mere act of violence.

As investigators pieced together the narrative, other details emerged that added complexity to the case. The Shermans, known for their relaxed security habits, often left some windows open and doors unlocked. Notably, the basement door, a potential point of discreet entry for someone familiar with the layout of the property, was often unsecured.

Further intriguing details surfaced regarding the whereabouts of the Shermans' personal items. Honey's iPhone was discovered in a seldom-used powder room, situated conveniently near the side door through which she typically entered the house. This placement led to the hypothesis that Honey may have rushed into this room upon encountering an intruder.

In a similar vein, during the fateful house tour, the real estate agents stumbled upon a stack of papers and Barry's gloves scattered on the floor. This scene, suggestive of a sudden disturbance or attack, was inadvertently altered when the realtor, unaware of the gravity of the situation, moved these items onto a nearby shelf, inadvertently contaminating what was soon to be identified as a crime scene.

Another compelling piece of evidence was the discovery of substantial cash in the wallets of the deceased couple, totaling almost $8,000. This discovery further contradicted the theory of a robbery gone awry. If theft had been the motive, it was unlikely that such a significant amount of cash would have been left untouched. This detail, combined with the other unusual aspects of the scene, strengthened the hypothesis that the Shermans had been the targets of a planned and deliberate attack, rather than victims of a random or opportunistic crime.

Dissatisfied with the pace and direction of the Toronto Police Department's investigation, the Sherman family took matters into their own hands. They hired a private detective to conduct an independent probe and enlisted a retired forensic pathologist to perform a second autopsy on the couple. This move underscored the family's determination to unearth the truth behind their parents' tragic end.

In January 2018, just over a month following the grim discovery, the case took a significant turn. While the Toronto Police were still classifying the deaths as "suspicious," the private investigative team reached a startling conclusion. They posited that Barry and Honey Sherman were murdered after being bound and strangled with belts. This chilling revelation shifted the narrative from ambiguity to a more sinister interpretation of events.

Subsequently, the Toronto Police Department altered its stance, acknowledging the case as a double homicide stemming from a targeted attack on the Shermans. This change in the official position marked a crucial development in the investigation, aligning more closely with the findings of the private investigators.

In October 2018, in an effort to galvanize the stalled investigation, the Sherman family announced a substantial reward of $10 million for information leading to the resolution of the case. This amount was later increased dramatically to $35 million in December 2022, reflecting both the family's commitment to finding answers and the enduring complexity of the case.

Since the deaths, a plethora of theories and speculations have emerged, with many veering into the realm of the outlandish, often centering around financial motives or vendettas.

One prominent theory involved the pharmaceutical industry. Given Barry's extensive legal entanglements and aggressive business tactics, there was speculation that forces within the industry, weary of his litigious nature, may have sought to end his influence permanently. Others surmised that competitors in the generic drug market, frustrated with Apotex's dominance under Barry's leadership, might have had a motive to remove him from the scene. However, these theories, while provocative, lack substantive evidence.

Another angle of speculation focused on the long-standing familial strife, particularly with Barry's cousin, Kerry Winter, and, to some extent, speculation around the Shermans' son, Jonathon. It is important to note that neither has been officially named as a suspect by law enforcement.

Kerry Winter, one of the four brothers who had previously sued Sherman over the sale of their father's company, had been particularly vocal about his animosity towards Barry following their legal defeat. He even made a startling claim that, in the 1990s, Barry had approached him — then a drug addict with criminal connections — with a request to arrange Honey's murder.

Despite failing a lie detector test regarding this allegation, Kerry's troubled history with Barry, characterized by bitterness and contentiousness, did not translate into concrete evidence of his involvement in the Sherman murders, according to police investigations.

The spotlight, at various points, turned towards the Shermans' son, Jonathon, particularly in light of a significant financial matter. Reports emerged of a $50 million loan that Barry had reportedly requested his son repay shortly before the couple's deaths. Jonathon vehemently denied that this financial issue was a source of contention, stating emphatically in 2021, "I'm not going to kill my dad because he needs $50 million to get through a crisis." However, he did acknowledge a rift within the family, particularly with his sister Alex, who had accused him of being involved in their parents' deaths, a charge he adamantly denied.

In 2022, further underscoring his commitment to finding the truth behind his parents' tragic end, Jonathon contributed an additional $25 million to the already substantial reward for information leading to a resolution of the case. His poignant statement highlighted his deep sense of loss and the haunting impact of the unresolved nature of his parents' deaths: "My parents deserved to enjoy the fruits of their labor, and spend their twilight years as any grandparent should, with their family. I continue to miss my parents more than I can describe, and I am forever haunted by what happened to them."

The case also saw theories veering into the realms of antisemitism and other conspiracy theories. Honey Sherman's sister put forth a theory that the Shermans were targeted due to their prominent roles and fundraising efforts within the Jewish community, speculating an antisemitic motive behind their deaths. She further suggested that Barry had been involved in efforts to disrupt funding channels to Muslim terrorist organizations.

Other conspiracy theories ranged from a Russian mob hit linked to a supply of fentanyl to outlandish speculations that Barry had been stockpiling hydroxychloroquine in anticipation of a global pandemic, a theory that lacked any credible evidence.

On December 21, 2022, the case saw a significant development when Toronto homicide detectives executed a new search warrant at an undisclosed location. This operation led to the acquisition of 14,801 electronic files containing previously unseen material. The contents of these files, however, remain largely under wraps, with only redacted portions made public.

The police, in their warrant, indicated that they were seeking documents and data that could either implicate or exonerate current persons of interest and shed light on potential motives for the murders. Det. Const. Dennis Yim, the primary homicide officer on the case, stressed the importance of keeping the documents sealed to prevent potential perpetrators from gauging the progress of the investigation.

Kevin Donovan, an investigative journalist with the Toronto Sun, hinted that the backup documents for the warrant might offer crucial clues. Interestingly, the focus of the investigation appears to have shifted towards Sherman's non-Apotex business ventures, particularly investments in the holding company, Sherfam. This angle remains a subject of ongoing scrutiny, with the Sun actively challenging the sealing order in court.

In a surprising twist in 2023, a French woman named Christelle Chaubet claimed to be Barry Sherman's biological daughter and accused Toronto Police of overlooking a vital lead she had provided regarding a potential suspect in the murders. Chaubet, a teacher in Toulouse, sought legal intervention from Ontario's Divisional Court to compel the police to investigate her allegations. According to court documents, Chaubet insisted that Sherman was her father and that she possessed information about a suspect that the Toronto Police had failed to pursue. Her numerous complaints to the Office of the Independent Police Review Director (OIPRD) underscored her claims of police inaction, adding yet another layer to the already complex and multifaceted investigation into the deaths of Barry and Honey Sherman.

Winnipeg Serial Killings

I n a chilling series of events that shook Canada, Jeremy Skibicki faced charges for the heinous murders of four Indigenous-Canadian women. This horrifying case unfolded in the early months of 2022, with the victims identified as Rebecca Contois, Morgan Harris, Marcedes Myran, and an unidentified woman, poignantly referred to as Mashkode Bizhiki'ikwe, or Buffalo Woman. The timeframe for these brutal acts was narrowed down to between March and May 2022, marking a dark period in Canadian history. However, as the case developed, no concrete citations were immediately available to substantiate these claims.

Further deepening the grim narrative, CBC News spearheaded an investigation into Skibicki's past. This probe unearthed a disturbing pattern of spousal abuse. Allegations surfaced that two of Skibicki's former partners, both of whom shared Indigenous (Métis) heritage, had suffered at his hands through assault, threats, and even rape. This information added a harrowing layer to an already complex and tragic case.

But the revelations didn't end there. A delve into Skibicki's social media footprint, particularly his Facebook activities, painted a picture of an individual entrenched in extreme ideologies. His posts and interactions were rife with far-right rhetoric, blatant misogyny, violent sentiments, anti-Semitic views, and white supremacist ideologies. These alarming discoveries, though currently without direct citations, added a concerning dimension to the understanding of Skibicki's mindset and possible motivations.

In response to these atrocious killings, the Canadian political arena was stirred into action. The House of Commons, recognizing the severity of the situation and its broader implications, initiated an emergency debate. This discussion was not just about the murders themselves, but also addressed the larger, ongoing epidemic of violence targeting Indigenous women and girls across the nation.

A significant outcome of this debate was the proposal and unanimous adoption of the "Red Dress Alert" by MP Leah Gazan. This initiative, directly referencing the murders and cited in a letter to Public Safety Minister Marco Mendocino, aimed to address and mitigate the risks faced by Indigenous women and girls. The Red Dress Alert became a symbol of awareness and action against this deeply rooted issue.

As the 2023 Manitoba general election approached, the case of Skibicki and his victims played a pivotal role. The ruling Progressive Conservatives faced criticism for their stance against searching the Prairie Green Landfill for the remains of Myran and Harris. This decision became a contentious issue in the political discourse. In contrast, the New Democrats, recognizing the public's outcry and the need for closure for the families of the victims, pledged to initiate the search if elected. This promise resonated with the electorate, contributing to the Progressive Conservatives' eventual defeat in the election. The aftermath of this case continued to ripple through Canadian society, highlighting the need for greater protection and justice for Indigenous women and girls.

The tragic tale of Jeremy Skibicki's alleged victims unfolds with a heart-wrenching narrative, deeply rooted in the indigenous community of Canada. Among the four individuals believed to have fallen prey to his heinous acts, three were confirmed Indigenous women, while the fourth, also suspected to be of Indigenous descent, remains shrouded in mystery. Each of these women, connected by their heritage, unfortunately shared a common vulnerability – several were reported by their family members to be homeless at the time of their disappearance, adding a layer of societal tragedy to their stories.

Rebecca Contois, a vibrant young woman just 24 years old, hailed from the O-Chi-Chak-Ko-Sipi First Nation. At the time of her disappearance, she was residing in Winnipeg, a city she called home. Her youthful life was cruelly cut short, leaving a void in the hearts of those who knew her.

Morgan Beatrice Harris, 39, also had her roots in the Long Plain First Nation. Like Contois, Winnipeg was her home city. Harris was last seen in the bustling area of Winnipeg's Main Street and Henry Avenue, a place where her presence is now sorely missed.

Marcedes Myran, another young woman from the Long Plain First Nation, was just 26 years old when she vanished. She, too, lived in Winnipeg, last seen in the city's North End neighborhood. Her disappearance left a gaping hole in her community and among her loved ones.

The fourth victim, known as Mashkode Bizhiki'ikwe or Buffalo Woman, remains unidentified but is believed to have been in her mid-twenties and living in Winnipeg. Initially referred to as "Jane Doe" or simply as an unidentified victim, her story took a poignant turn when advocates and Indigenous elders came together to bestow upon her the name "Buffalo Woman." This name, rich in cultural significance, was adopted by the Winnipeg police in a gesture of respect and acknowledgment. It symbolizes the buffalo spirit, traditionally given to those who had not received a spirit name, ensuring their recognition in both the physical and spirit realms. Distinctively, Buffalo Woman was thought to have donned a Baby Phat brand reversible jacket, characterized by a fur hood, a detail that perhaps offers a glimmer of her personal style and identity.

These women, tragically linked by their untimely deaths, represent more than just victims; they are a stark reminder of the vulnerabilities faced by Indigenous women and the ongoing struggle for safety and recognition within their communities. Their stories, laden with sorrow, continue to resonate deeply, prompting conversations and actions towards change and justice.

Jeremy Anthony Micheal Skibicki stands accused of a series of profoundly disturbing crimes, casting a long shadow over the Canadian judicial landscape. He faces charges of first-degree murder in the deaths of four individuals: Rebecca Contois, Marcedes Myran, Morgan Harris, and the woman known as Buffalo Woman. In a move that adds yet another layer to this complex and harrowing case, a representative for Skibicki has asserted that he will plead not guilty to all charges.

Skibicki's past is marred by a troubling history of alleged violence and abuse, particularly towards his partners. In June 2015, he was convicted following a horrific assault on his then common-law partner, who was pregnant at the time. In a shocking display of brutality, Skibicki strangled and repeatedly punched the woman in the face, coupling these violent acts with a chilling threat to kill her if she sought police assistance. Despite the gravity of these actions, a protection order filed by the woman was subsequently dismissed. The case reveals a pattern of violent behavior, as Skibicki not only expressed violent fantasies towards a previous partner but also allegedly smothered her to the point of causing her teeth to bleed. His sentence for this assault was two months in prison, followed by two years of probation.

The cycle of abuse continued into 2019, when Skibicki's then-wife sought a protection order against him on their first wedding anniversary. By 2021, the situation had escalated alarmingly. Skibicki faced charges for disobeying court orders, making threats, and assaulting her with a deadly weapon. His threats were of a particularly sinister nature, including statements of intent to kill, torture, traffic, or abduct her. She reported enduring horrific abuse at his hands, including being raped while asleep and suffocated with a pillow. In May 2022, amidst these tumultuous and violent circumstances, his wife initiated divorce proceedings. Another charge of assault against Skibicki, allegedly for attacking his spouse, was stayed. Notably, both of Skibicki's former partners shared Indigenous Métis heritage.

The dark portrait of Skibicki is further painted by findings from a CBC News investigation into his online activities. His personal Facebook page was a hotbed for disturbing content, including material that was violently antisemitic, misogynistic, and white supremacist in nature. Skibicki's self-identification with groups espousing extreme ideologies adds a concerning dimension to his profile. He described himself as a member of "Holy Europe" and the "Alliance of Patriotic Parallel Movements of European Folks" (APPMEF). This organization is deeply entrenched in far-right ideology, advocating for the preservation of white European bloodlines against perceived threats from race-mixing, multiculturalism, and immigration.

In sum, the case of Jeremy Skibicki, marked by allegations of brutal violence and underpinned by extremist ideologies, presents a stark and troubling chapter in Canada's criminal justice narrative, highlighting issues of domestic abuse, racial tensions, and the dark underbelly of far-right movements.

The earliest suspected murder is that of the woman known as Buffalo Woman, believed to have been killed on March 15, 2022. This date marks the beginning of a series of events that would later horrify the nation. Around this same time, Marcedes Myran lost contact with her family, a silence that would later be understood in the most tragic of contexts.

Investigators pinpoint May 1, 2022, as the day Morgan Harris was likely killed. This date corresponds with the last known sighting of Harris alive, intensifying the mystery and urgency of the case.

The timeline suggests a rapid succession of events, with police suspecting that Myran was murdered just days later, on May 4, 2022. The delay in reporting her missing, not until September 26, 2022, speaks volumes of the family's trepidation and the hope against hope that she might still be safe.

Rebecca Contois is believed to have been the last victim, with police alleging her murder occurred between May 14 and 15, 2022. The discovery of her partial remains on May 16, 2022, in a garbage bin near an apartment complex in Winnipeg's North Kildonan neighborhood, was a gruesome find that shook the community. This discovery led to a broader search, culminating on June 2, 2022, with the unearthing of further remains belonging to Contois at the Brady Road Landfill.

In the wake of these discoveries, Skibicki was charged on May 18, 2022, for the murder of Contois, setting in motion the legal proceedings against him. Meanwhile, the search for other victims continued, with authorities issuing an alert on May 24, 2022, seeking assistance in locating Harris.

The case took a significant turn on December 1, 2022, when police announced additional charges against Skibicki for the first-degree murders of Harris, Myran, and Buffalo Woman. The following day, Skibicki appeared in court, with the decision being made to bypass a preliminary hearing and proceed directly to trial.

The discovery of Rebecca Contois' partial remains on May 16, 2022, marked a harrowing chapter in the investigation of her disappearance. The scene, described as "horrifically grisly," was located in the garbage bins behind Mar Joy Apartments in the North Kildonan area of Winnipeg. This grim discovery led to the realization that some of Contois' remains might have been inadvertently transported to the Brady Road landfill as part of the regular residential garbage collection process.

In a solemn and respectful gesture, authorities initiated a search at the Brady Road landfill for the rest of Contois' remains on June 2, 2022. This search began with the lighting of a sacred fire, reflecting the cultural sensitivities and profound nature of the task at hand. The search team included authorities from Ka Ni Kanichihk's Medicine Bear Counselling Program and the Manitoba Keewatinowi Okimakanak's unit for missing, murdered Indigenous women and girls, underscoring the collaborative effort in this tragic situation. The search efforts bore fruit on June 21, 2022, when some of Contois' remains were discovered at the landfill.

Meanwhile, the Prairie Green Landfill emerged as another critical location in this complex investigation. It was suspected that the remains of both Marcedes Myran and Morgan Harris were located there. In June 2022, the landfill was briefly closed, a fact that remained undisclosed to the public until revealed by a group overseeing a feasibility study on the recovery of the remains. On June 20, 2022, homicide investigators concluded that it was likely that the remains of Myran and Harris could be found in the Prairie Green Landfill.

However, the prospect of conducting a search at the Prairie Green Landfill for Myran and Harris faced significant challenges. On December 6, 2022, police announced that such a search might not be feasible. This announcement was followed by a call from Premier Heather Stefanson to pause operations at the landfill on December 8, 2022. Subsequent developments saw only a single cell's activities being paused, as announced on December 15. In a significant move, the federal government declared on the same day that it would cover the costs for an Indigenous-led feasibility study regarding the recovery of the remains at the landfill. Premier Stefanson pledged support for this study the next day, reflecting a growing recognition of the importance of this issue.

The Assembly of Manitoba Chiefs, responsible for overseeing the feasibility study, expressed optimism about the possibility of conducting a search. They indicated that the search could potentially begin as early as April 2023, offering a glimmer of hope in the midst of a deeply tragic and complex situation.

The discovery of Linda Mary Beardy's body at the Brady Road Resource Management Facility on April 4, 2023, ignited a new wave of concern and speculation. A member of the Lake St. Martin First Nation, Beardy had lived in Winnipeg before her untimely death. Her body was found in a location disturbingly close to where some of Rebecca Contois' remains were previously discovered, which initially raised suspicions of a possible connection to the series of deaths linked to Jeremy Skibicki. This proximity to the site where other victims were found brought renewed urgency from the families of Skibicki's victims, who called for thorough searches of the nearby landfills.

However, the investigation into Beardy's death took a different turn. The Winnipeg Police, after gathering witness accounts, concluded that Beardy was not a victim of homicide. Witnesses reported seeing her climb into a garbage bin, which was subsequently collected by a truck, hours before her body was discovered. Police Chief Danny Smyth stated that there were no indications of foul play. This conclusion, however, was met with skepticism and criticism from Beardy's family, who expressed dissatisfaction with the transparency and thoroughness of the Winnipeg Police's investigation.

In the midst of this tragedy, Winnipeg Mayor Scott Gillingham acknowledged the deep impact of these events, stating that mere condolences were insufficient. He recognized that the women involved were integral members of the community, highlighting their roles as daughters, sisters, mothers, and friends. Gillingham's comments at a press conference underscored the need for more significant efforts in protecting Indigenous women and girls, pointing to the vulnerabilities created by factors such as homelessness, addiction, and poverty.

In response to the ongoing crisis of missing and murdered Indigenous women, girls, and two-spirit people (MMIWG2S+), Members of Parliament Leah Gazan (Winnipeg Centre) and Niki Ashton (Churchill—Keewatinook Aski) advocated for an emergency debate in the House of Commons of Canada. They called for increased resources and support for vulnerable women in light of Skibicki's alleged crimes. Unfortunately, their request for a debate was not granted, leading Gazan to criticize the government's slow response in providing necessary resources, emphasizing the ongoing danger faced by Indigenous women, girls, and two-spirit individuals.

Gazan also pressed Marc Miller, the Minister of Crown–Indigenous Relations, on the Winnipeg Police's decision not to search the Brady Road landfill for the bodies of the three missing Indigenous women. Miller expressed his puzzlement over the decision and conveyed his intention to meet with Harris's family. Meanwhile, Gazan, along with other Indigenous leaders, met with the families of Harris and Wilson in a press conference, demonstrating a concerted effort to address these deep-seated issues and advocate for those most vulnerable.

Dorothy Scott

On the morning of August 6, 1984, a chilling discovery was made in the quiet town of northeast Anaheim, California. Just half a mile east of the serene Eucalyptus Drive, a scene that seemed straight out of a mystery novel unfolded. It was around 7:15 a.m., a time when the sun had just started to cast its warm glow over the landscape, that Jesse Loza, a seasoned foreman with Macco Construction Company, came across a shocking sight. While he and his diligent crew were preparing the grounds to lay telephone lines for Pac Bell, an unexpected and macabre find halted their work.

In a twist that seemed like cruel irony, just minutes after Loza had lightheartedly warned his crew to "watch out for dead bodies," his jest turned into a grim reality. There, amidst the underbrush, lay the partially charred remains of an adult human skeleton. This gruesome find was not alone; alongside it was the partial skeleton of a dog, weaving an even more intriguing and sorrowful story.

The scene, as described by Richard Rodriguez, the Deputy Coroner for Orange County, painted a picture of a tragic and mysterious incident. The initial theory suggested that perhaps the individual, accompanied by their loyal canine companion, had been out hiking when an unforeseen calamity struck them down. The exact cause of their demise remained shrouded in mystery, with the coroner listing it as "questionable."

Further examination revealed that the remains were scattered across a 25-

foot radius, a detail that hinted at the likelihood of animal scavenging activity over time. Adding to the complexity of the case was the burnt condition of the bones. This crucial clue led investigators to link the remains to a brush fire that had ravaged the area in the fall of 1982. This connection provided a tentative timeline, suggesting that the bones had been lying undiscovered at this lonely spot for over two years.

As the investigation progressed, the team meticulously collected what remained: a complete skull, two femurs, a pelvis, an arm, and the bones of the dog. The location of this grim find was peculiarly juxtaposed with the trappings of civilization. Encircled by housing tracts, the site overlooked the bustling Riverside Freeway and was situated merely 30 feet from the well-traveled Santa Ana Canyon Road. This proximity to everyday life, coupled with the length of time the remains had gone unnoticed, added an eerie layer to the unfolding mystery.

In the sun-drenched expanse of Anaheim, California, a story unfolded that was as enigmatic as it was tragic. The year was 1984, a time marked by neon lights and an era of change, but in the quiet outskirts of northeast Anaheim, time seemed to stand still as investigators unearthed a haunting discovery. The bones, bleached white from their long exposure to the relentless California sun, told a silent tale of mystery and sorrow. Among these skeletal remains, a skull stood out, complete and eerily intact, housing a full set of teeth riddled with fillings – silent witnesses to a life once lived. Richard Rodriguez, the seasoned deputy coroner, announced plans to scour the missing person's database, hoping these dental records would unlock the identity of the deceased.

Enter Judy Suchey, an esteemed anthropologist from Cal State Fullerton. Her expertise was sought to unravel the enigma of the remains – to deduce the age and sex of this person who had been claimed by time and elements.

The twist in the tale came when the remains were identified as those of Dorothy Jane Scott, who had vanished into the night four years prior. At the time of her disappearance, Dorothy was a 32-year-old single mother, devoted to her four-year-old son. She was the epitome of love and kindness, described by her friends and family as a beacon of warmth and generosity. Dorothy's life was simple yet full; her world revolved around her son, her faith, and her close-knit family. She and her son resided in Stanton, California, with Dorothy's aunt, Shonti Jacob Scott, a mere 20-minute drive from where her parents lived in Anaheim and where she worked.

Her workplace, Swingers Psych Shop and Custom John's Head Shop, was once under the ownership of her father, Shawn Scott, but had since been acquired by John Kocyla. The shops, with their eclectic and vibrant nature, were a stark contrast to the quiet life Dorothy led. Her father, a familiar figure around the businesses, was known and liked by all who worked there.

The tranquility of Dorothy's life was shattered in early 1980 when she began receiving unsettling phone calls at work. These calls, filled with intimate details of her daily life, were from an anonymous stalker – a man whose voice seemed hauntingly familiar to Dorothy, yet she couldn't place it. His words fluctuated between declarations of love and dark, vengeful threats. The situation escalated when Dorothy found a dead rose on her car windshield – a chilling symbol of the stalker's presence in her life.

One phone call, in particular, stood out for its sheer terror. The stalker's menacing voice declared, "OK, now, you are going to come my way, and when I get you alone, I will cut you up into bits so no one will ever find you" (The Orlando Sentinel, 1984). This threat sent shivers down Dorothy's spine and pushed her to consider arming herself for protection. However, instead of opting for a firearm, she decided to empower herself through karate classes, a decision that spoke volumes about her character – one that chose strength and resilience over fear.

The day was May 27, 1980, a seemingly ordinary day with the California sun casting its warm glow over the city. Dorothy Scott had a simple plan for the day

- drop her beloved son off at her parents' home and head to a work meeting. Little did she know that this day would mark the beginning of a perplexing and haunting chapter in her life.

As Dorothy attended her work meeting, she noticed something amiss about her co-worker, Conrad Bostron. His hand had been inflamed due to a spider bite, and he appeared unwell. Being the caring and compassionate person that she was, Dorothy, along with another co-worker named Pam Head, offered to take Conrad to the hospital for treatment. Conrad, grateful for their help, agreed, and the three of them embarked on a journey in Dorothy's white 1973 Toyota Station Wagon. Their destination: UCI Medical Center.

Before heading to the hospital, they made a quick detour to Dorothy's parents' home to inform them of the situation. During this visit, Dorothy even took a moment to change the headscarf she was wearing, a seemingly insignificant detail that would later take on a puzzling significance.

Upon arriving at the hospital, Conrad received the necessary treatment for his black widow spider bite. While he recuperated, Pam and Dorothy passed the time by watching TV and flipping through magazines, completely unaware of the sinister turn their day was about to take. As Conrad was released from the hospital around 11 p.m., Pam and he headed to the hospital pharmacy to fill his prescription. Meanwhile, Dorothy, always considerate of her friends, decided to go to the parking lot to retrieve the car, ensuring that Conrad wouldn't have to walk far.

However, it was at this point that Dorothy's story took a chilling twist. She never returned to the entrance where Pam and Conrad awaited her. The minutes turned into hours, and growing concern gave way to panic. Conrad and Pam decided to retrace their steps, making their way to the spot where Dorothy's car had initially been parked. To their astonishment and alarm, they saw Dorothy's white Toyota Station Wagon hurtling toward them with blinding high beams, its driver obscured from view. Instead of stopping or slowing down, the car simply veered onto the road and sped away, leaving them bewildered and anxious.

They waited for what felt like an eternity, speculating that an emergency involving Dorothy's son had arisen. But as time wore on, it became increasingly clear that something was terribly wrong. Worried and baffled, they contacted hospital security, hoping for answers, but none were forthcoming. The last memory they shared with Dorothy was her brief restroom visit just before heading to the parking lot. Her sudden disappearance left them in a state of shock and disbelief.

Desperation set in, and they reached out to Dorothy's parents, hoping for some insight into her whereabouts. However, her parents had not heard from her either, and a sense of dread began to envelop them all. It was at this moment that they realized Dorothy was missing, and their frantic search for answers began.

The evidence of foul play emerged when, in the early hours of the following morning, Dorothy's car was discovered engulfed in flames in an alley roughly 10 miles from the hospital. The inexplicable circumstances surrounding her disappearance deepened the mystery, and fear gripped Dorothy's loved ones.

About a week after Dorothy's abduction, her mother, Vera, received a chilling phone call from her daughter's stalker. The voice on the other end of the line inquired, "Are you related to Dorothy Scott?" With trepidation, Vera confirmed their relationship. What followed was a bone-chilling revelation as the stalker declared, "I have her," before abruptly hanging up. This terrifying encounter left Dorothy's family in no doubt that something sinister had befallen their beloved daughter.

Desperate for answers and driven by their unwavering love for Dorothy, her parents, Vera and Jacob Scott, decided to take their daughter's story to the local newspaper. They offered a substantial $25,000 reward, hoping that it would yield leads and shed light on the perplexing case of their missing daughter. The saga of Dorothy Scott's disappearance had captured the imagination of a community and had all the makings of a harrowing mystery that would persist for years to come.

The date was June 12th, 1980, a day that would forever be etched in the memory of Pat Riley, the editorial manager for the Santa Ana Register. On that fateful day, Riley received a chilling phone call that would thrust him into the heart of a perplexing and haunting mystery. The voice on the other end of the line was calm, yet filled with an eerie determination. The man on the phone claimed to have committed a gruesome act.

What made this call all the more spine-tingling was the knowledge possessed by the caller. He revealed details that had never been made public, details that only someone intimately familiar with the events of that night could know. He knew about Conrad's spider bite, an incident that had occurred during their ill-fated trip to the hospital. He even knew about the subtle change in Dorothy's headscarf, the one she had swapped just before heading to the hospital, a detail seemingly insignificant but now imbued with sinister meaning.

The caller's narrative took a disturbing turn when he claimed that Dorothy had called him from the hospital. This assertion was perplexing and at odds with the accounts provided by Pam, who had been with Dorothy throughout that fateful night at the hospital. Pam adamantly stated that Dorothy had not made any such call. It raised the chilling possibility that the caller's version of events existed solely within the dark recesses of his mind. In the absence of modern communication devices like cell phones or pagers in 1980, any call made by Dorothy would likely have been from one landline to another, most likely a home phone. The timing of such a call, given the circumstances, appeared implausible. It hinted at a level of obsession and delusion that defied comprehension.

In the aftermath of this disturbing call, the case entered a period of eerie silence. For the next three years, Dorothy's tormentor would sporadically make phone calls to her parents, further deepening the mystery. The police, desperate to trace the location of Dorothy's abductor, tapped the phone line in the hope of a breakthrough. However, the calls were always brief, and the stalker never stayed on the line long enough to be traced. Curiously, it seemed that Dorothy's stalker had now turned his attention to her parents, targeting them with his unsettling calls. Strangely, he would only make contact when Vera, Dorothy's mother, was home alone. Then, in a strange twist, the calls abruptly ceased when Shawn Scott, Dorothy's father, answered the phone. They remained silent until the grim news broke that Dorothy's remains had been discovered, at which point the calls resumed, with the eerie inquiry, "Is Dorothy home?" before hanging up. The Scotts made the heart-wrenching decision to never change their phone number, holding on to the hope that one day, they might have the chance to speak with their missing daughter.

In the absence of solid leads, the case presented a frustrating enigma. Dorothy, by all accounts, was a homebody who spent her time either at home with her son, in the company of family, or at work. Her regular attendance at church painted a picture of a woman deeply rooted in her community. Even her former partner, the father of her son, was swiftly eliminated as a suspect, as he was in Missouri at the time of her abduction.

However, a glimmer of hope and suspicion arose in 2017 when a crime blogger conducted an interview with Shawn Scott, Dorothy's son. In this conversation, he named the brother of one of Dorothy's co-workers as a person of interest. According to those familiar with the pair, this individual had exhibited an unsettling obsession with Dorothy. Shawn went on to claim that law enforcement had kept a close eye on this individual but had never been able to amass enough evidence for an arrest or charges. Tragically, this alleged suspect passed away in 2014, taking his secrets to the grave.

The passage of time cast a long shadow over the Scott family, bringing both closure and unanswered questions. In 1994, on what would have been Dorothy's birthday, her father, Jacob Scott, passed away. Vera Scott, Dorothy's mother, followed in 2002, a staggering 22 years after her daughter's abduction. Their hearts forever carried the weight of not knowing what happened to Dorothy or who was responsible. The case, despite the passage of decades, remains stubbornly unsolved, a testament to the enduring mystery surrounding the disappearance of Dorothy Scott.

Dean and Tina Clouse

In the quaint, sun-kissed town of New Smyrna Beach, Florida, two young hearts, Harold Dean Clouse Jr. and Tina Gail Linn, found each other amidst the serene backdrop of the late 1970s. Their story began in 1978, in a place where the salty sea air mixed with the dreams of youth. Tina, a mere 15 years old, brimming with the innocence of teenage years, met Dean, a 19-year-old with a gentle demeanor, whose sister was romantically involved with Tina's brother – a relationship that later blossomed into marriage.

Their love story was nothing short of a fairy tale. Those who knew Dean and Tina often reminisced about their "whirlwind romance", a term that aptly described the rapid and passionate way in which their love unfolded. In a testament to their profound affection, the couple, unable to wait any longer, tied the knot in a modest but heartfelt ceremony at the Volusia County Courthouse on the warm summer day of June 25, 1979.

The following year, on January 24, 1980, their love was further solidified with the birth of their daughter, Holly Marie. Those who surrounded the young family often spoke of Dean and Tina as devoted parents, each moment with Holly cherished and filled with love.

As the 1980s dawned, the Clouse family found themselves yearning for a new beginning. Thus, in the summer of 1980, they embarked on a journey to the bustling suburb of Lewisville, Texas, located in the thriving Dallas metropolitan area. The Dallas-Fort Worth region at the time was a land of opportunity, buzzing with rapid development and a booming construction industry. Dean, with his adept skills as a cabinet maker, saw this as a golden opportunity to provide for his young family and sought to make a mark in the thriving trade.

Upon arriving in Texas, the family initially stayed with Dean's cousin, a move that was both strategic and familial, allowing them to save for a home of their own. Dean soon found employment with D.R. Horton homebuilders, a testament to his skill and dedication in his craft. Despite the challenges of finding stable work in those early days in Texas, the couple maintained a harmonious relationship, as observed by those who knew them.

In the autumn of 1980, Dean and Tina Clouse's lives took a mysterious and tragic turn. Having recently embarked on a new chapter in Texas, the young couple suddenly and inexplicably ceased all communication with their families around late October, mere months after their relocation. This sudden silence cast a shadow of worry and uncertainty over their loved ones.

The grim truth of their fate would not be revealed until several weeks later. It is now believed that their untimely deaths occurred sometime between October 1980 and January 1981. On the chilling winter day of January 12, 1981, their decaying bodies were discovered, marking a tragic end to their young lives. The last known sighting of the Clouses alive was in Lewisville, Texas. However, the circumstances of how they ended up over 250 miles away in the desolate and swampy woodlands north of Houston remain shrouded in mystery.

In 1981, as months drifted by without a word from Dean and Tina, Dean's mother, Donna Casasanta, filed a missing persons report. However, the initial police investigation was lackluster, hindered by a prevailing belief that the couple had intentionally severed ties. This belief was partly fueled by the enigmatic return of their car to Florida, reportedly by members of an unidentified nomadic religious group. Despite these setbacks, their families tirelessly pursued grassroots efforts to find them, including reporting the disappearance to the Salvation Army, known for keeping tabs on missing persons. Unfortunately, these efforts bore no fruit, and no information from the Salvation Army's database made its way into federal databases of missing people.

The discovery of their bodies was as macabre as it was heartbreaking. On January 12, 1981, in a boggy, wooded area of northern Harris County, Texas, just beyond the Houston city limits, the remains of Dean and Tina Clouse were found. This gruesome discovery was initiated by a civilian's dog, which disturbingly returned to its owner with a decomposing human arm. Prompted by this horrifying find, search parties scoured the area and eventually came upon the heavily decomposed bodies of the Clouse couple, lying close to each other near Wallisville Road. The state of the bodies suggested they had been dead for several weeks, if not months, with Dean's remains partially skeletonized.

Despite the advanced state of decomposition, enough features remained for facial reconstructions to be drawn. Autopsies revealed a violent end: Tina had been strangled, while Dean had been bound, gagged, and beaten to death. It was speculated that Tina was attacked first, with Dean falling victim in a desperate attempt to defend her. Among the clues found at the scene were a bloodied towel and a pair of gym shorts, adding to the mystery of whether the couple was killed at the location or brought there post-mortem.

The investigation into the mysterious and tragic deaths of Dean and Tina Clouse proved to be a complex and challenging endeavor, with very few leads emerging beyond the initial evidence collected at the grim discovery site. Early assessments mistakenly categorized the victims as teenagers or young adults, a detail that underscored the difficulty in identifying them. The prevailing theory at the time was that Tina had been the initial target of the attack, with Dean tragically losing his life in a valiant attempt to protect her.

In an effort to uncover the victims' identities, Harris County forensic artist Mary Mize painstakingly created facial reconstructions of both individuals. However, these artistic endeavors, although skilled, failed to shed light on the identities of the deceased. This lack of recognition was later attributed to the fact that the Clouses, having recently relocated to Texas, had not yet established significant connections in the area, rendering them virtually unknown in the local community.

With their identities remaining a mystery, the couple was interred in the Harris County Cemetery, known only as the "Does." The case, despite the sorrowful story it told, began to grow cold, with no arrests made in connection to the murders even after the Clouses were eventually identified.

The case, however, saw a resurgence of hope and activity in July 2011, decades after the couple's untimely demise. In a significant development, the bodies were exhumed for the extraction of DNA. This crucial step was initially aimed at determining if the victims were related, a detail that could provide a pivotal clue in unraveling their identities.

The opportunity for exhumation arose when Harris County received a grant from the National Institute of Justice. This funding was part of a larger initiative to exhume several unidentified murder victims, including the Clouses, for the purpose of extracting and analyzing their DNA. This data would then be entered into national databases, potentially opening new avenues for investigation.

Overseeing this crucial phase was Jennifer Love, the forensic anthropology director of the identification unit in the Harris County medical examiner's office. Her expertise and leadership would prove instrumental in the renewed efforts to solve this perplexing case.

In an unexpected twist, the investigation received a boost from an unlikely source: the true crime podcast company Audiochuck. Their interest in the case led to the securing of additional funding for continued genealogical research into the Harris County Does.

The intricate puzzle of identifying the Harris County Does took a promising turn in late 2020 when the case was handed over to Identifinders International, a California-based genetic genealogy organization renowned for its expertise in unraveling complex DNA mysteries. The organization's approach combined cutting-edge genetic analysis with traditional genealogical research, offering a glimmer of hope in a case that had long remained shrouded in mystery.

The task of uncovering the identities of the Does fell to forensic genealogists Misty Gillis and Allison Peacock, who embarked on a meticulous journey through the labyrinth of genetic data. Utilizing Gedmatch, a genetic database renowned for its comprehensive ancestry information, Gillis and Peacock divided their focus; Gillis concentrated on the male DNA, while Peacock delved into tracing the female's lineage.

Gillis's investigation into the male's DNA yielded several distant matches leading to Kentucky. This crucial clue steered her towards a family with the surname Clouse, who had roots in Kentucky but had subsequently moved to Florida. Persistently tracing the Clouse family's genealogical tree, Gillis eventually stumbled upon an extremely close DNA match to the male victim.

In a parallel effort, Peacock, acting as the representative for both her and Gillis, reached out to Debbie Brooks, the sister of Dean Clouse. She inquired if Debbie's family had lost any member over 40 years ago. This conversation opened a new chapter in the investigation as Brooks provided vital information about her brother Dean, enabling the genealogists to identify Dean Clouse Jr. within a mere 10 days of initiating their research. Tina Clouse's identification followed shortly thereafter, thus resolving the mystery of the Harris County Does within weeks of the case's reopening.

The revelation of Dean and Tina Clouse's identities was publicly announced by the Texas Attorney General's cold case unit on January 12, 2021, marking the 40th anniversary of the discovery of their remains. Until this moment, Donna Casasanta, Dean's mother, had clung to a faint hope that her son might still be alive.

Following these groundbreaking identifications, Allison Peacock continued her involvement with the case, serving as a public relations liaison and advocate for the Clouse family. Her role transcended the boundaries of forensic genealogy, embodying a commitment to providing support and closure to the bereaved family.

In a poignant tribute to their lost loved ones, families of both Dean and Tina traveled to Houston. They visited the haunting location where the bodies were discovered and paid their respects at the gravesites. During this solemn journey, Les Linn, Tina's brother, shared that both families had reached a touching consensus: to have Dean and Tina laid to rest together.

The identification of Dean and Tina Clouse marked a significant breakthrough in a long-standing mystery, but it also opened a new, equally perplexing chapter: the search for their missing daughter, Holly Marie. No evidence of a baby's body was found near the couple's remains, and no fitting baby Doe cases had ever come to light. This absence of clues led to a bewildering question posed by Debbie Brooks, Dean's sister, during a conversation with Allison Peacock: "What baby?" Peacock's unawareness of Holly Marie at that moment underscored the complexity and gaps in the case.

Theories about Holly Marie's fate varied widely. Some speculated that her small body might have been carried away by scavenging animals, while others wondered if she could have been overlooked at the crime scene. However, the most chilling and increasingly accepted theory was that Holly Marie had been abducted by her parents' killer or killers. This theory gained traction when it was revealed that Holly Marie had been left at a church in Arizona by two women dressed in white robes and barefoot, claiming to be part of a nomadic religious group, shortly after her parents' murders.

The efforts to find Holly Marie intensified with Allison Peacock and her organization, FHD Forensics, joining forces with the Clouse and Linn families. The Hope For Holly DNA Project was launched, disseminating information about Holly's last known location and releasing an age-progressed image crafted by the National Center for Missing and Exploited Children. In a bid to find a genetic match, several family members submitted DNA samples to genealogy websites. The search was vast and complex, with numerous women across the country contacting Peacock, believing they might be Holly. Each potential lead was meticulously tested and ruled out, showcasing the dedication and thoroughness of the search.

The remarkable discovery of Holly Marie Clouse came on June 7, 2022, in Oklahoma. Remarkably, this was also Dean's birthday, a poignant coincidence in this extraordinary story. The long-held hypothesis that Holly, if alive, would be unaware of her true identity proved correct. The investigation into her disappearance was complicated, with different agencies involved and confusion over the spelling of her name. A significant breakthrough occurred when investigators discovered that her birth certificate had been sealed due to adoption.

While respecting Holly Marie's privacy, it has been shared that she led a contented life, complete with a 20-year marriage, five children, and two grandchildren. Details of her childhood remain confidential due to the ongoing investigation into her parents' deaths, with her adoptive family never considered suspects. The church that initially took Holly in had facilitated her adoption to a family who was unaware of the mysterious circumstances surrounding her arrival.

The reunion of Holly Marie with her biological family was both heartwarming and surreal. They first met virtually over Zoom on the day she was found and later in person in Florida, thanks to funding from NCMEC.

In the aftermath of Holly Marie's safe recovery, the Hope for Holly Project evolved into the Dean and Tina Linn Clouse Memorial Fund, redirecting its focus to aid in identifying other unidentified decedents. The growth of this initiative led to the creation of Genealogy For Justice™, a 501c3 charity, in October 2022. The organization, advised by members of the Clouse and Linn families and genealogist Peacock, achieved a significant milestone on Mother's Day 2023, identifying Virginia Higgins Ray as a Jane Doe from 1982 in Columbia, South Carolina.

The ongoing investigation into the tragic murders of Dean and Tina Clouse remains a critical and active criminal case, as confirmed by Harris County Police Deputy Thomas Gilliland. The case, shrouded in part by restrictions due to its active status, continues to intrigue and challenge investigators. With the recent developments and the return of Holly, the long-cold case has seen a resurgence of interest, leading to a fresh influx of leads that are being pursued by the Texas Attorney General's cold case unit.

Central to the mystery surrounding the Clouse murders is the involvement of a religious group, a thread in the case that adds layers of complexity and intrigue. The 1970s, a time marked by the emergence of "Jesus freak" movements, provided fertile ground for the formation of cults. These movements, though waning in relevance by the 1980s, were characterized by their unorthodox practices and often radical beliefs. Dean, according to his family, had past interactions with such movements during his teenage years, but had distanced himself from them after his relationship with Tina Linn began.

An enigmatic figure known as "Sister Susan" emerged in December 1980, a period now believed to be close to the time of the Clouses' murders. Sister Susan, claiming to be part of a religious group, made contact with the couple's family in Florida, expressing an intention to return Dean and Tina's car. By then, the couple had already been out of contact with their family for several weeks. A peculiar meeting was arranged at Daytona Racetrack in Florida, shrouded in secrecy and taking place under the cover of night. Sister Susan, accompanied by other group members who remained silent, communicated to the family that Dean and Tina had joined their group and chosen to cut off worldly ties.

Adding to the strangeness of the encounter, the group requested a $1,000 donation from Donna Casasanta, Dean's mother. Despite the family's suspicion and the presence of police notified in advance, no formal report of the incident appears to have been filed.

When Donna Casasanta later attempted to report her son as missing, the police quickly dismissed her concerns, citing the return of the car and Sister Susan's claims as evidence of Dean's voluntary disappearance. The Clouse families, however, never believed that Dean and Tina would willingly join a cult, and it is now suspected that the car's return was a calculated move to deter a formal investigation.

The religious group involved in these perplexing events is also believed to be the same one that left Holly at a church in Arizona. Described as living a nomadic lifestyle across the Southwest United States, their practices included male and female separation, vegetarianism, and the avoidance of leather goods. Intriguingly, this group was also reported to have abandoned another baby in the past, this time at a laundromat. The involvement of this group adds a profound layer of mystery to the case, intertwining the Clouses' fate with the enigmatic and unconventional practices of a religious group that remains shrouded in secrecy and suspicion.

Chase Massner

In the warm glow of early September 1987, Chase Tyler Massner entered the world, the son of youthful parents, Corbin Massner and Stephanie Cadena. Both barely stepping into their twenties, the couple's journey together was fleeting, parting ways as Chase grew.

Chase's childhood, shrouded in the mists of time, emerges into clarity with a single blemish: an arrest for marijuana possession in August 2005. At eighteen, his mugshot captured a young man unaware of the profound transformations that lay ahead. This minor scrape with the law, fortunately, did not derail his ambitions, paving the way for him to fulfill a cherished dream—serving in the United States Army.

The late 2000s witnessed Chase's evolution from civilian to soldier, a journey that took him across the globe to the war-torn landscapes of Iraq. Upon his return, the invisible scars of post-traumatic stress disorder, as later recounted by his wife Amanda, began to surface.

Love blossomed amidst these turbulent times, with Chase marrying Amanda shortly after his return. The couple welcomed their first beacon of joy, Sydney, into their lives, but the shadow of Chase's parents' fragmented past loomed over them, a history they desperately hoped not to repeat. Yet, life had other plans, weaving a tapestry of complexities that would later challenge any effort to unravel the truth.

Chase's familial bonds painted a picture of warmth and support. His mother, Stephanie Cadena, a long-time employee at a family-owned auto repair company, shared a bond with Chase that epitomized the ideal mother-son relationship. In times of strife with Amanda, Chase often sought refuge and counsel at his mother's side.

Conversely, the relationship with his father, Corbin Massner, remained an enigma, a puzzle piece that would later prove critical in understanding Chase's story. Corbin, a truck driver who moved in with Chase's family following a job loss, added to the mounting financial pressures faced by Chase and Amanda.

Post-military life was a relentless struggle for Chase. He juggled various jobs, striving to provide for his family. The arrival of their second child only intensified their financial woes. In a bid to keep the family afloat, Chase took up a night manager position at a Quik-Trip in Kennesaw, Georgia, a stone's throw from his friend Brad Clement's residence.

The Massner family home in Canton, Georgia, stood as a testament to their struggles—a modest abode for a family of four, five with Corbin's inclusion, sustained on a meager hourly wage. Questions swirled about how they managed, hinting at a fortuitous housing deal, yet the reality of their financial tightrope walk was palpable.

Amidst this backdrop of financial strain and reversed schedules, the fabric of Chase and Amanda's marriage began to fray, strained under the weight of responsibility and unending hardship, setting the stage for events that would soon catapult their lives into an unforeseen and tragic trajectory.

In the spring of 2014, the fabric of Chase and Amanda Massner's marriage was fraying at the edges. Their home had become a battleground of escalating disputes, with Chase often seeking refuge and counsel from his mother, Stephanie Cadena. Stephanie, in her role as mediator and confidante, oscillated between offering advice over the phone and providing Chase a temporary haven at her home, giving the couple much-needed breathing space.

This delicate balance of intervention and retreat was put to the test one particular day in March. Amanda, overwhelmed by the mounting pressures and incessant quarrels, reached out to Stephanie. Their conversations revealed a tangled web of financial strain and emotional turmoil, but both women agreed it wasn't a chasm too vast to bridge. The decision was made: Chase would spend a few nights at his mother's house, a temporary retreat to quell the storm and reset their strained relationship.

March 26th dawned with a poignant farewell, as Chase, surrounded by his children's eager faces, bid goodbye to his mother. Unbeknownst to Stephanie, this parting glance would etch itself as her final memory of her son.

The narrative then veers into a labyrinth of conflicting accounts and blurred truths. The central figures in this unfolding drama are Chase's wife, Amanda, and a friend from his past, Brad Clements. The journey back from Stephanie's home, meant to be a path to reconciliation, quickly devolved into renewed conflict. The argument escalated rapidly, casting a shadow over any hopes of a peaceful resolution. Whispers and rumors swirl about the nature of this dispute, with some suggesting Amanda asked Chase to leave the car. What is known is that Chase ended up at the Quik-Trip where he worked, miles away from the sanctuary of his home in Canton.

In the tapestry of Chase Massner's life, James Bradshaw Clement, known to his friends as Brad, emerges as a curious figure. Their friendship, its origins as elusive as the morning mist, was a bond forged in the familiar landscapes of Atlanta, Georgia. Both roughly the same age, Brad and Chase shared a hometown, but the intricacies of their connection remained a mystery. They had met a handful of times, leaving one to ponder the threads that drew them together.

Nestled about half an hour north of the bustling heart of Atlanta, in the quaint town of Kennesaw, was where Brad called home. This serene suburb, a stark contrast to the urban sprawl of Atlanta, boasted scenic forests and a charming downtown, a world away from the city's clamor. It was here, in Kennesaw, that Brad carved out a life for himself, working with computers, repairing them in the sanctuary of his home. Rumors had it that he was also employed by T-Mobile at the time, but the truth of his professional life remained as shadowy as the story itself.

Brad's abode, a handsome house at the end of Farmbrook Trail's cul-de-sac, stood as a testament to his self-made success. Despite the whirlwind of events that would later engulf his life, Brad retained an air of normalcy, a regular guy caught in an extraordinary saga.

The narrative takes a turn on the day Amanda, Chase's wife, dropped him off at the Quik Trip near Brad's residence. That evening, Chase sought solace in Brad's company. As the hours slipped by, they delved into conversations about life, love, and the tumultuous tides rocking Chase's marriage. Brad, in a twist of fate, stepped into the role of mediator, channeling his efforts through a flurry of text messages sent to Amanda from Chase's phone. His messages, a blend of concern and camaraderie, hinted at plans for a barbecue, a hopeful gesture to mend fences with grilled delights.

The following morning, March 27th, dawned with Brad poised to deliver a computer to a client. As he left, he made an unusual decision – to take Chase's cell phone with him. This phone, doubling as Chase's wallet, was his lifeline. Brad's rationale was steeped in good intentions; by holding onto Chase's phone, he believed he could anchor his friend at his home, a sanctuary from the storm of his life.

This choice, seemingly benign, cast a shadow of peculiarity over the unfolding story, adding another layer of complexity to a narrative already shrouded in enigma. The path from here only grew more tangled, the facts and fictions intertwining, leading deeper into the labyrinth of Chase Massner's mysterious circumstances.

The enigma surrounding Chase Massner's final hours hinges precariously on the credibility of Brad Clements' account. As the last known person to see Chase, Brad's testimony forms the backbone of a story mired in uncertainty and suspicion.

Brad's recollection of the day Chase disappeared paints a picture of ordinariness tinged with peculiar decisions. He had, in a move to ostensibly keep Chase from leaving, taken his friend's cell phone while running errands. His narrative unfolds with a return to find Chase still at his home, followed by a departure to gather supplies for a planned barbecue. It was during this window of time, Brad asserts, that Chase vanished.

Skepticism naturally clouds Brad's version of events. Questions arise: Was Brad's account accurate? Did he withhold details or alter facts?

In a revealing interview on Nancy Grace's podcast, Brad delves into the evening prior to Chase's disappearance, describing a scene where alcohol and marijuana blurred the edges of reality. He also drops a bombshell, claiming Chase was on the lookout for "roxy" pills, a street name for the opiate painkiller roxicodone. This revelation potentially pivots the investigation, suggesting a desperate quest for drugs, fueled by a maelstrom of personal issues, from strained relationships to the haunting specter of PTSD.

Brad maintains his distance from this world of substance misuse, despite admitting to previous encounters with roxicodone following a car accident. Yet, his claim of giving Chase $60 prior to his disappearance raises eyebrows and ignites speculation. What was the intent behind this financial gesture? Was it an innocent act of friendship, or something more sinister?

Media coverage, often frenzied and speculative, has largely sidestepped Brad's narrative, focusing instead on casting him as a dubious character. This rush to judgment obscures a vital fact: Brad's testimony is the only thread investigators have to weave together the final day of Chase's life. His words, whether taken at face value or scrutinized for hidden meanings, are the key to unlocking the mystery of what truly happened to Chase Massner.

During the crucial days surrounding Chase Massner's disappearance, Brad Clement's home, the epicenter of the mystery, was undergoing renovations. The focus was on the roof, being replaced by Ducks Roofing, a local business run by Brandon Duck. Brad's home buzzed with activity as Brandon and his crew worked through the day.

Brad, having left to run errands, returned to a house alive with the sounds of construction and the anticipation of an upcoming barbecue. The roofers recall seeing him both in the morning and upon his return, noting their planned participation in the cookout. It was during these preparations that Brad encountered an unexpected mishap: a fire in his backyard, ignited accidentally during grill setup. After extinguishing the flames, Brad re-entered his home, expecting to share the incident with Chase, only to find his friend mysteriously absent.

This disappearance occurred in broad daylight, raising questions about its unnoticed nature. Brad's home, situated at the end of a cul-de-sac, would have made any departure of Chase visible, yet no one reported seeing him leave. The enigma deepened when Brandon Duck and his crew, who had been present throughout the day, revealed they had no recollection of seeing Chase at all. This glaring inconsistency cast a shadow of doubt over Brad's account, particularly as he later attributed the discrepancy to a miscommunication. The perplexity surrounding this explanation, how someone could report the departure of a person they never knew was present, only added to the growing web of confusion.

Amidst these puzzling circumstances, the search for Chase Massner was set into motion, a quest for truth in a sea of uncertainties and contradictions.

The narrative, marked by questionable testimonies and unclear sightings, encapsulated the complexity of a mystery that was only just beginning to unravel.

The mystery of Chase Massner's disappearance began to ripple outward, reaching his family even before Brad Clement made his call to Chase's phone. The sequence of events, like a complex game of telephone, left Brad under the impression that Amanda, Chase's wife, had picked him up. However, the reality was murkier, as revealed in a phone call from Stephanie Cadena, Chase's mother, placed just fifteen minutes prior to Brad's call. In a voice tinged with concern, Stephanie expressed her growing anxiety over Chase's whereabouts, having learned that he hadn't returned home with Amanda the night before.

As the puzzle pieces began to shift, Amanda and Stephanie reached out to Brad, who maintained that Chase had left his house that afternoon, supposedly seen by the roofers—a claim later proven false. Efforts to trace Chase's steps intensified, with calls made to his friends and acquaintances, but each inquiry led to a dead end.

In Brad's neighborhood, no one remembered seeing Chase that day. While it's not unusual for residents to overlook the comings and goings within their vicinity, especially during the quiet hours of early afternoon, the complete lack of sightings seemed implausibly rare.

Chase had vanished, leaving behind no clues, no witnesses, and an increasingly desperate family. When the police were finally called in, they approached the case as a voluntary disappearance, operating under the assumption that Chase had chosen to leave of his own accord. This perspective, while standard in such cases, added another layer of frustration for those who knew Chase and believed that something more sinister might have unfolded. The search for answers continued, shrouded in uncertainty and the haunting question: what really happened to Chase Massner?

Three years after Chase Massner's disappearance, one aspect that continually casts a shadow over the investigation is the initial handling of the case by the Cherokee County police force. Chase lived in Canton, Georgia, with his family, situating the responsibility of the investigation on the local police. However, these circumstances often lead to critical details slipping through the cracks, as was highlighted in my coverage of the Long Island Serial Killer cases, where jurisdictional issues complicated the investigations.

The complexity in Chase's case was compounded by his last known location in Kennesaw, Georgia, falling under Cobb County's jurisdiction. This geographical overlap led to initial investigative hurdles. A significant setback was the Cherokee County police's approach to Chase's disappearance as a voluntary absence, implying they believed he had chosen to leave on his own.

In his interview on Nancy Grace's podcast, Brad Clement suggested that Chase had spoken about running away to live in the woods. While this claim remains uncorroborated by others, it seemingly influenced the police's perspective, leading them to downplay the potential severity of the situation.

As time passed, the likelihood of Chase's voluntary departure began to wane. He had his debit card and cell phone with him, but the last transaction on his debit card occurred on March 26th, the evening he went to Brad's house. The nature of this small purchase remains unknown, potentially as mundane as buying a snack or a soda.

Chase's cell phone usage ceased after March 27th, the day of his disappearance, with his last call made the previous night. The fate of his phone, much like Chase himself, remains a mystery. There are conflicting accounts about its whereabouts, with some suggesting Brad had it all day, while others imply Amanda may have possessed Chase's old phone following an upgrade.

These uncertainties provided little assistance to law enforcement. Even when the urgency of the investigation ramped up and the case was transferred back to Cobb County police, the jurisdiction where Chase actually vanished, all tangible traces of him had seemingly evaporated. The investigation into Chase Massner's disappearance, fraught with jurisdictional entanglements and conflicting testimonies, became a journey through a fog of uncertainties, leaving more questions than answers in its wake.

Brad Clement and Amanda Massner, Chase's wife, have both faced intense scrutiny and backlash in the wake of Chase's mysterious disappearance. Amanda, in particular, became a prime suspect in the court of public opinion due to conflicting accounts she provided about the night of March 26th, the last time she was with Chase.

Stephanie Cadena, Chase's mother, remembers Amanda initially saying she dropped Chase off at the Quik Trip where he worked. Yet, there was also talk of Amanda leaving Chase directly at Brad's house, adding layers of confusion and suspicion to her narrative.

Amanda's plight intensified as she navigated the aftermath of Chase's vanishing. Her interactions were closely examined, including a phone call where she discussed the scrutiny she faced in the weeks and months that followed. This scrutiny wasn't just from the public or the authorities; Brad Clement himself cast aspersions on her character.

In a startling turn, Brad alleged in an interview with Nancy Grace that Amanda had approached him the day after Chase disappeared. He insinuated that she was not only seeking marijuana but also appeared to be flirting with him, possibly as a retaliatory gesture against Chase. Brad further claimed that Amanda was involved in her mother's marijuana cultivation operation, though he offered scant details to substantiate this accusation.

Amidst this turmoil, Amanda's own words added complexity to her situation. In a conversation with a veteran's group mobilizing to search for Chase, Amanda's comments were ambiguous, leaving listeners uncertain whether she was referring to Chase's issues with marijuana or heroin. This revelation was a jarring contrast to the positive image often portrayed in missing persons reports, yet such personal struggles could provide crucial leads in understanding his disappearance.

The audio also highlighted Amanda's gradual retreat from public life. Initially active in the search for Chase, she became increasingly reclusive, eventually leaving Georgia and severing communication with the media and others involved in the case.

A significant factor in Amanda's withdrawal was her involvement with Paul Libri, a private investigator in Georgia. She entrusted him with aiding in the search for her husband, unaware of his dubious background. Paul Libri was later convicted of impersonating a police officer and other charges related to a separate missing person's case. This betrayal of trust likely contributed to Amanda's decision to isolate herself and relocate to Iowa with her daughters, distancing herself from the ongoing saga and the pain it brought.

In the immediate aftermath of Chase Massner's disappearance, Brad Clement did not fall under police suspicion. The investigation, initially framed as a case of voluntary departure, did not implicate Brad in any wrongdoing. However, the situation around Brad began to evolve as new details emerged.

Police requested Brad to undergo a polygraph test, which he declined, citing his anxiety and questioning the test's reliability. Indeed, the efficacy of polygraphs as truth detectors is debatable, as they measure stress responses rather than veracity. Concerns about the phrasing of questions and the potential for false positives are valid. For instance, an innocent person might still exhibit a strong stress response to an accusatory question, skewing the results. Brad's reluctance to take the test, therefore, was understandable.

Suspicion around Brad grew when it was discovered that he had a dumpster outside his home, where he was having renovation work done. Friends and family of Chase urged the police to investigate this dumpster, believing it could hold crucial evidence. The police eventually conducted a search, but a critical error was made: they examined the wrong dumpster. By the time this mistake was realized, the correct dumpster had already been emptied into a landfill. The cost of searching the landfill was prohibitively high, and the likelihood of finding relevant evidence after such a delay was minimal.

This mishap added to a series of errors that plagued the investigation, diminishing its integrity. Despite these developments, Brad was never officially named a suspect by the police. However, public opinion shifted dramatically against him. The story of the misplaced dumpster and Brad's inconsistent alibi cast a shadow of doubt over his character. He faced intense public scrutiny and backlash, eventually leading him to leave his home and the area where he grew up. His move came just months after Chase's disappearance, and his only notable public appearance since then was in an interview with Nancy Grace.

The turning point in the investigation came with the unearthing of human remains in Brad's former backyard. This discovery seemed to validate the suspicions many had harbored. On August 23rd, 2017, it was confirmed that the body found was indeed Chase Massner.

In a surprising twist, Brad, who had sold his home and lived a somewhat transient life after Chase's disappearance, suddenly went on the run. He had previously maintained his innocence in interviews, but his flight cast doubt on his assertions. Brad was eventually apprehended in DeKalb County, Georgia, after a week-long manhunt. Found in a white van in a Publix parking lot, he was arrested and charged with concealing a death. His criminal record in the intervening years, including charges of forgery and heroin possession, further complicated his situation.

As the case continues, Brad has not yet been charged with Chase's murder. It's important to remember that the legal process must be respected and that

Brad remains innocent until proven guilty. However, this development brings a somber closure to the search for Chase Massner. It's a tragic ending for a man who was a father, husband, soldier, and son. The discovery offers some resolution to the Massner and Cadena families, and it's hoped that they can find some measure of closure in this heartbreaking conclusion. Our thoughts remain with them during this difficult time.

Carol Cole

In the quaint town of Kalamazoo, Michigan, the lives of two sisters, Carol Cole and Linda "Jeanie" Phelps, took a dramatic turn following their parents' divorce. The siblings found themselves under the nurturing care of their grandmother, a shift that marked the beginning of a series of events that would later become shrouded in mystery and intrigue.

Carol, the elder of the two, embarked on a life-altering journey in 1979, at the tender age of 15. She made the bold decision to leave the familiar streets of Kalamazoo and join her mother, Sue, in the bustling city of San Antonio, Texas. Despite the physical distance, Carol maintained a strong bond with her sister Linda, keeping the lines of communication open through regular phone calls, painting a picture of her new life miles away.

In a twist of fate, Carol found herself at a girl's home run by the Palmer Drug Abuse Program (PDAP) on West 23rd St. in Austin, Texas, between May and October 1980. This period marked a significant chapter in her life, one filled with the challenges and complexities of adolescence. Carol continued to reach out to her family, sending letters filled with thoughts and experiences, a lifeline that unexpectedly ceased in late December 1980.

The mystery deepened when Carol's grandmother, back in Kalamazoo, traced her granddaughter's steps to a house in Shreveport, Louisiana, after Carol left PDAP. It was here that the grandmother encountered a chilling revelation: Carol had left to attend a party but never returned. This news set off alarm bells, prompting Linda Phelps and her friend Patty Thorington to launch a relentless search for Carol, a quest fraught with dead ends and unanswered questions.

Adding to the enigma, a medical examiner had previously ruled out Carol as a possible identity for an unidentified victim, leaving more questions than answers. Rumors and speculations swirled, with some sources suggesting that Carol may have spent time at a religious institution, the New Bethany School for Girls in Arcadia, Louisiana. This lead gained traction when Linda recalled an image from around the time of Carol's disappearance, showing a group of girls in pews, one strikingly similar to her sister.

The investigation took various turns, with leads and sightings adding layers to the mystery. A woman came forward, claiming to have spent time with a girl resembling Carol but couldn't recall her name. Theories abounded, including speculation that the names written on the victim's shoes and her clothing style might link back to the dress code of the New Bethany School for Girls.

On the fateful day of January 28, 1981, a harrowing discovery was made in the secluded woods of Bellevue, Bossier Parish, Louisiana. Hidden among the trees lay the body of a young female, her life tragically cut short. Estimated to be between 15 and 21 years old, this Jane Doe presented a mystery wrapped in enigma, her identity obscured by the veil of death.

Clad in jeans and a white, long-sleeved shirt adorned with pink, yellow, and blue stripes, she lay there in her beige hooded sweater, her attire reflecting the casual fashion of a youthful spirit. Her feet were shod in shoes that bore intriguing names: "Michael Brisco", "David", "Resha", and "D. Davies". These names, etched on her shoes, whispered tales of companionship, yet led nowhere in the quest to uncover her story. White socks with blue and yellow streaks, white boxer briefs, a white bra, and a leather belt with a distinctive "Buffalo Nickel" buckle completed her ensemble, each item a silent witness to her untold story.

Her fingernails, painted prior to her death, hinted at a life once lived with attention to detail and personal care. The shoes she wore, size seven, were ordinary yet crucial clues in piecing together her last moments. Near her remains, a knife was found embedded in the soil, a grim reminder of the brutality she faced: she had been stabbed nine times, a cruel end to a young life.

The tragedy was compounded years later when, in 2005, a fire ravaged the facility housing much of the evidence, erasing crucial clues that might have led to her identity or her killer.

The investigation into her death painted a portrait of a young woman of average build, about 5 feet 5 inches to 5 feet 6 inches tall, weighing between 125 and 140 pounds. Though decomposition had obscured much of her appearance, she was believed to be white, possibly with Native American ancestry. Her hair was described as blonde, straight, and shoulder-length, but the color of her eyes remained a mystery, lost to time and decay.

A peculiar detail emerged about her dental history: she had once had orthodontics, but the braces appeared to have been removed, either by herself or by someone with no professional expertise. This detail added another layer of intrigue to her story.

The case took a bizarre turn when convicted killer Henry Lee Lucas confessed to her murder, only for it to be later proven impossible; Lucas was in Florida at the time of her death, and he was known for his pattern of false confessions.

In an effort to give her a face, investigators first created a three-dimensional clay model, and later, with advances in technology, a digital reconstruction was made by the Louisiana State University FACES Lab. As science progressed, DNA was eventually extracted from her teeth, providing a glimmer of hope that one day, it might match a missing person's profile, bringing closure to a case that had long remained cold.

In the midst of uncertainty and despair, Jeanie Phelps, Carol Cole's devoted sister, took decisive action in the face of her sibling's mysterious disappearance. With a heavy heart and a growing sense of dread, Jeanie filed a missing person's report for Carol. Despite harboring suspicions of foul play, she clung to the hope of finding her sister. The case was entered into the National Missing and Unidentified Persons System (NAMUS), casting a wider net in the desperate search for Carol.

Undeterred, Jeanie, along with Carol's childhood friend, turned to the power of social media in their quest. They utilized platforms like Facebook and Craigslist, not just as tools for communication, but as beacons of hope, broadcasting Carol's story far and wide in the hope of gathering any leads or information. Meanwhile, the grandmother who had once fiercely pursued Carol's whereabouts passed away, leaving Jeanie to carry the torch of this relentless search.

In a parallel effort, on February 6, 2015, the local sheriff's department in Bossier Parish launched a unique initiative. They created a Facebook page dedicated to identifying the unknown young woman, who had by then been nicknamed "Bossier Doe". This digital appeal quickly garnered attention, with over five hundred people connecting with the "Bossier Doe" account in just a few days. The number of followers soared to over a thousand in less than a week, illustrating the power of community engagement in the digital age.

This digital outreach took a dramatic turn when Linda Erickson, a 911 operator, chanced upon the Facebook page featuring Bossier Doe's image. In a moment of serendipity, Linda recognized a striking resemblance between the image and a photo of Carol Ann in a Craigslist ad. This ad, a heartfelt plea for information, was posted by Patty Thorington, a friend of Carol's sister. Within days, Patty received a crucial email from the Sheriff's Office, linking Carol to the Bossier Doe case.

The breakthrough led to a pivotal moment in the investigation. DNA tests were conducted, comparing the victim's profile with that of Carol's parents. The results were conclusive: Carol and "Bossier Doe" were one and the same. This revelation prompted a surge of support, culminating in the creation of a GoFundMe account to cover the expenses for a new burial and headstone, as Carol's family faced financial challenges in transporting her body and commemorating her life.

On June 18, 2015, Carol was laid to rest in Maple Grove Cemetery in Comstock Township, Michigan, following a heartfelt funeral service. Her identity now known, the investigation shifted its focus to finding the person responsible for her tragic end.

In a startling development, Frances Aucoin, whose father, John Chesson, had discovered Carol's remains alongside her brother, came forward with a chilling suspicion. She believed her father, already incarcerated for life for a separate murder, was involved in Carol's death. Chesson, a figure marred by a history of violence and the murder of his estranged wife's mother, became a person of interest. Aucoin's account painted a harrowing picture of her father's character, suggesting he had brought a young woman resembling Carol into their home after picking her up as a hitchhiker. Her brother, another witness in the grim discovery of Carol's body, tragically took his own life in 2008, adding another layer of tragedy to this complex case.

As the investigation continues, the quest for justice for Carol Cole persists, a testament to the enduring hope and resilience of those who loved her and the relentless pursuit of truth by law enforcement.

Keddie Murders

In the heart of Springfield, Massachusetts, on a crisp spring day in 1945, a new chapter began with the birth of Glenna Susan Davis. From her earliest days, she was affectionately known by her middle name, Sue. A name that would, in time, become synonymous with resilience and courage.

Sue's journey through life took a turn when she crossed paths with James Sharp, a young man whose presence would shape her destiny in ways she could never have imagined. Their union blossomed into a bustling household of seven, with the pitter-patter of three boys, John, Rick, and Greg, and the gentle laughter of two girls, Sheila and Tina. The rhythms of military life meant a nomadic existence for the Sharp family, with Sue anchoring their world as a devoted stay-at-home mother.

However, the winds of change were blowing. After a move from Connecticut to the sun-soaked Carolinas, Sue's marriage began to unravel. Dark clouds hovered as she faced the harrowing truth of James' abusive behavior, a reality that threatened the very fabric of their family. Summoning her inner strength, Sue made the brave decision to leave James, embarking on a journey to safeguard her five precious children.

Their odyssey led them across the American tapestry, eventually finding solace in the embrace of northern California. Here, in this land of new beginnings, Sue's brother, Don Davis, stood as a beacon of hope and support in the quaint area of Quincy.

As fate would have it, Sue and her children found themselves drawn to the rustic charm of Keddie, a once-thriving resort town now echoing with the memories of its past glory. Nestled in the mountains, this small town, with its rich history and scenic beauty, offered a fresh start for the Sharp family. Sue rented a cabin in what was once the bustling Keddie Resort, now a haven for those seeking a new start.

Cabin 28, a humble abode amidst the mountain air, became a sanctuary for the Sharps. With its two bedrooms, it was a cozy nest for the family, offering a space for each child to call their own. It was in this modest cabin that the Sharp family began to weave their new life together, surrounded by the natural splendor of the mountains.

As 1981 dawned, Sue and her children embraced their new community with open arms. Sue, ever resourceful, balanced part-time work at a nearby lodge with support from social programs and a military stipend. Her pursuit of education at Feather River College further fueled her determination to provide for her family. Despite the absence of support from James, Sue's tenacity ensured that her family never lacked for love and care.

In this tight-knit community, Sue was known for her warmth, yet she cherished her privacy, often found at home, a quiet sentinel for her children. Meanwhile, the Sharp kids thrived in their new environment, making friends and becoming well-known figures in their local school.

On the cusp of spring, April 11th, 1981 dawned as a serene Saturday, cloaking the Sharp household in Keddie with an air of normalcy and tranquility.

That morning, as the sun gently warmed the earth, Sue Sharp and her daughter Sheila, a sprightly 14-year-old, embarked on a short journey to Quincy, the nearby town that served as the hub of local life. Their mission was simple: to fetch 15-year-old John, who was enjoying the day with his friend, 17-year-old Dana Wingate, a local high schooler with a reputation for stirring the pot.

The afternoon waned, and around 3:30 PM, John and Dana ventured back out, drawn to the allure of Quincy and its promise of adolescent adventures. They planned a return home later that evening, with Dana intending to stay over. Sue, ever the protective mother, warned against hitchhiking, her words falling on the rebellious ears of youth.

John and Dana, familiar figures in the small town tapestry of Quincy, were seen meandering through its streets that afternoon, their presence a common thread in the community's fabric.

As the sun dipped lower, rumors whispered of a clandestine party attended by the boys, shrouded in secrecy and the shadowy allure of teenage rebellion. The specifics of this gathering remained cloaked in mystery, dissuaded witnesses holding their tongues in the face of underage indulgences. The boys were last glimpsed hitchhiking in the cool embrace of the evening, their journey home shrouded in unknowns.

Meanwhile, the Sharp cabin, nestled in the heart of Keddie, hummed with the ordinary rhythms of a Saturday night. Sheila, the doting mother, spent the afternoon with Tina, her 12-year-old daughter, while her two youngest, Rick and Greg, enjoyed the companionship of Justin Eason, a neighborhood friend, in anticipation of a sleepover.

The evening unfolded quietly, with Sue holding the fort at home. Tina and Sheila ventured next door to Cabin 27, the home of the Seabolt family, their newfound friends in the close-knit community. The girls, drawn by the allure of television and friendship, spent their evening there, with Tina returning home around 9:30 PM to surrender to slumber.

Sheila, however, remained at the Seabolts', her night spent in the warmth of a sleepover with her friend Alysa. This simple decision, unbeknownst to her, would become a pivotal moment in her life, a guardian against an unknown fate awaiting at home.

As the night stretched on in the quiet enclave of the Keddie Resort, a resident was stirred awake by unsettling sounds, a mix of groaning and muffled screams, between 1:00 and 2:00 AM. But the stillness soon returned, and the darkness held its secrets.

The dawn of April 12th, 1981, brought a horrifying revelation to 14-year-old Sheila Sharp. Leaving the neighboring cabin where she had spent the night, she approached her home, its door ajar as usual. But what lay beyond was a scene of unimaginable horror. The sight that greeted her was chilling: her brother John's lifeless body, bound and bloodied, lay closest to the door, amidst a scene of brutal carnage.

In a panic, Sheila fled back to the Seabolt residence, her screams piercing the morning calm. The Seabolts, James and Zonita, struggled to grasp the gravity of her words, their minds reeling from the grotesque description. They immediately sought help, while their teenage son Jamie was sent to check for survivors.

Jamie's cautious entry into the cabin revealed a startling contrast. In the back bedroom, young Rick and Greg Sharp, along with their friend Justin, lay sleeping, blissfully unaware of the nightmare unfolding mere feet away. Jamie, thinking quickly, guided the boys out through a bedroom window, sparing them the traumatic sight and preserving the integrity of the crime scene.

The call to the authorities was made around 8:05 AM from a nearby lodge, the Seabolts lacking a phone of their own. The Plumas County Sheriff's Office was swiftly mobilized, officers descending on the scene, their arrival coinciding with that of Sue's brother, Don Davis. Don, overwhelmed by grief and horror, struggled to identify the bodies amidst the grisly tableau.

As the morning progressed, the cabin became a hive of activity, with law enforcement meticulously documenting the extensive evidence. The crime scene was a testament to brutality: blood spattered across the walls, furniture, and even the ceiling; stab wounds marred the cabin's wallpaper, a chilling display of the killers' ruthless savagery.

Amidst the chaos and bloodshed, three lives had been brutally extinguished: John Sharp, the spirited 15-year-old; Dana Wingate, his 17-year-old friend with a penchant for trouble; and Sue Sharp, the 36-year-old matriarch who had fought so hard for her family's safety.

But a haunting realization soon dawned – 12-year-old Tina Sharp was nowhere to be found. Her absence, initially overlooked in the shock of the crime scene, became a pressing mystery. As the day wore on, the investigators worked tirelessly, sending the bodies for autopsy and piecing together the events of that fateful night.

The autopsies of Sue Sharp, her son John, and his friend Dana Wingate painted a grim portrait of their final moments, revealing a scene of relentless savagery that young Sheila would tragically stumble upon.

In a chilling detail, all three victims were discovered bound with electrical cords and medical tape, suggesting premeditation. Intriguingly, two different types of medical tape were used, hinting at the possibility of the materials being sourced from within the Sharp household.

The autopsies brought to light stark contrasts in the victims' final struggles. John and Dana bore no defensive wounds and no blood under their bindings, indicating they were likely restrained before the onslaught began. Sue's condition, however, told a different story. She bore the marks of a fierce resistance, with defensive wounds and blood found beneath her bindings, suggesting she was attacked while attempting to defend herself.

The bindings on Sue were noticeably tighter, and she had been cruelly gagged with a bandana and her own underwear, both pushed deep into her mouth and secured with tape. Her pants were removed, adding a disturbing layer to the scene, though there was no evidence of sexual assault.

Sue was found lying near the living room sofa, partially covered by a blood-soaked yellow blanket, a gesture that some speculate was an attempt to mask the brutality of the act. She had been stabbed multiple times and suffered blunt force trauma to the head, matching impressions from a Daisy 880 BB gun, a detail corroborated by a broken piece of the gun found at the scene.

John, found near the door, shared a similarly brutal fate. He had been stabbed, his throat slit, and had also suffered blunt force trauma, likely from a hammer.

Dana's body was discovered in a position suggesting a struggle, with evidence of both hammer-inflicted injuries and manual strangulation.

The investigators surmised that this heinous act was neither quick nor spontaneous. The perpetrator, or perpetrators, appeared to have spent a significant amount of time inside the cabin, executing their plan with chilling precision. Remarkably, the attack seemed to have occurred with minimal noise, as no witnesses came forward to report any disturbances.

Adding to the complexity of the scene, the investigators noted that both Sue's feet and one of the teenage boys' shoes were bloodstained, indicating movement through the bloody scene. The exact sequence of these movements remained an enigmatic piece of a puzzle that was as horrifying as it was baffling.

At the macabre scene in Cabin 28, the police uncovered a chilling array of weapons believed to have been used in the brutal attack. Among these were a hammer and a knife, both found near the victims, and a steak knife from the Sharp family's kitchen, warped grotesquely by the violence of its use. The bloodstains on these weapons painted a grim picture of their role in the crime.

The evidence suggested that the living room had been the primary stage for the murders, as indicated by the abundant blood and the stab marks scarring the walls. A startling discovery was made in 12-year-old Tina's room, where a trace of blood on her bed sheets hinted at a terrifying possibility – that she might have been sleeping during the murders and was subsequently abducted by the assailant. This raised an unsettling theory: the perpetrator might have been someone with intimate knowledge of the family, perhaps targeting Tina specifically.

In a town where trust and openness reigned, the lack of forced entry into the cabin was not surprising. The Sharps, like many in Keddie, rarely locked their doors, further easing the path for the assailant.

Post-murder, the cabin was found in a state of eerie calm, with lights turned off, blinds drawn, and the phone off the hook, a deliberate move to isolate the cabin from outside communication.

However, the investigation beyond the cabin's walls bore little fruit. The Seabolt family, residing in the adjacent Cabin 27 and hosts to Sheila on that fateful night, reported no unusual sights or sounds – a chilling testament to the stealth or familiarity of the perpetrator, given their proximity to the crime scene.

Other residents did report some unusual occurrences: one family recalled a faint sound resembling muffled screaming around 1:30 AM, while others noted suspicious vehicles, including a green van and a brown Datsun with a potentially flat tire, near the Sharp cabin. These sightings, however, failed to yield significant leads.

As the search for Tina Sharp intensified, the Plumas County Sheriff's Office faced criticism for their initial handling of the case. In the crucial early hours, there was a lack of awareness that Tina was missing, a lapse that cost precious time in a race against the clock to find her. This oversight underscored the department's inexperience with crimes of such gravity, and as hours turned into days, the trail to find the abducted 12-year-old grew increasingly cold.

At the heart of the investigation, police discovered a crucial clue amidst the chaos of the crime scene—a lone bloody fingerprint. This unidentified print, found on a post of the handrail leading to the cabin's back door, suggested the direction of the killer's escape. Years have passed, yet this fingerprint has not been matched to anyone, leaving a haunting question mark in the case.

The early days of the investigation were consumed by efforts to analyze this fingerprint, but detectives were soon awash in a sea of theories.

Central to the speculation were teenage victims John Sharp and Dana Wingate, last seen around 10:00 PM in Quincy, trying to hitchhike home against their mother's wishes. The identity of their driver remained a mystery, fueling theories that this individual could either be the killer or hold crucial information. Perhaps the boys were followed home, or the killer harbored a vendetta against one of them.

The party John and Dana attended on the murder night became a focal point. Don Stoy, a key figure in the investigation, later reflected on the party's potential drug connections and the reluctance of witnesses to come forward for fear of legal repercussions. This led to widespread rumors linking the murders to drugs, though concrete evidence was lacking. For instance, Carla McMullen suggested Dana stole LSD from local dealers, but this claim, like others, was unsupported by tangible proof. The Sharp cabin bore no signs of drug involvement or paraphernalia, debunking the drug-related murder theory.

Equally unsubstantiated were rumors of a Satanic ritual behind the murders. Authorities consistently dismissed these claims, believing the crime stemmed from personal motives. This theory posited that Sue Sharp might have been the primary target, with John and Dana tragically interrupting the attack.

This line of inquiry brought James Sharp, Sue's ex-husband, into the spotlight. Although his past abusive behavior raised suspicions, he had a solid alibi, clearing him of involvement in the murders.

Justin Eason, a neighbor of the Sharp family, found himself entwined in the tragic events at Cabin 28 in an unexpected way. On the night of the murders, Justin was having a sleepover with Rick and Greg Sharp, safely asleep in the back bedroom, untouched by the violence unfolding in the living room.

Initially, Justin, like the other boys, claimed to have slept through the entire incident, unaware of the horrors occurring just beyond their door. However, this account began to shift when Justin, under the care of a clinical psychologist, described vivid dreams that eerily mirrored the crime scene. These dreams included specific actions, like covering Sue Sharp with a blanket and trying to stop her bleeding, which raised questions among investigators, particularly when considering the presence of dried blood on the doorknob of the boys' bedroom.

In a bid to unlock hidden memories, Justin underwent hypnosis under the guidance of Sheriff Doug Thomas and Dr. Jerry Dash. The details he revealed during this session were both troubling and surreal. He recounted being on a boat with John Sharp and Dana Wingate, witnessing a physical altercation with an unidentified man, later amended to two men. His account, blending elements of a TV show he watched that night, "The Love Boat," with a dream-like narrative, painted a chaotic picture of the attack.

Justin's hypnotic testimony, though challenging to parse for its blend of dream and reality, resonated with some aspects of the crime scene. He spoke of attempting first aid on Sue, the sudden involvement of John and Dana, and Tina's emergence leading to her abduction.

The credibility of Justin's statements under hypnosis, however, was difficult to ascertain. Conducted a month after the murders, it was hard to determine if his accounts were influenced by news reports or local rumors. Moreover, the session transcripts indicated that Justin's responses often aligned with suggestions from Dr. Dash and Sheriff Thomas, raising questions about the reliability of his recollections.

Nevertheless, this session yielded a tangible outcome: descriptions of two potential suspects. These men, both in their late 20s or early 30s and wearing gold-framed sunglasses, differed in height and hair color—one with long, dark-blond hair and a mustache, the other shorter with greasy black hair.

These descriptions were converted into police sketches and widely circulated, drawing attention from the community. Despite multiple claims of recognition, no concrete suspects emerged. Intriguingly, locals noted that one of the sketches bore a striking resemblance to Marty, Justin's stepfather, adding a layer of complexity and suspicion to an already convoluted case.

Martin "Marty" Smartt, Justin's stepfather and a resident of Keddie, emerged as a figure of interest in the aftermath of the Cabin 28 murders. A Vietnam veteran grappling with PTSD and known for his deep-seated anger, Marty had notably developed a disdain for John Sharp, one of the teenage victims.

The day following the grisly discovery at Cabin 28, Marty was interviewed by law enforcement. His involvement in the investigation soon raised red flags; Sheriff Doug Thomas later observed that Marty seemed overly eager to divert suspicion from himself.

In his interview, Marty recounted spending time at Keddie's Back Door, a local bar, with his wife Marilyn and friend John Boubede, also known as "Bo." Curiously, he mentioned seeing two men at the bar who bore an uncanny resemblance to himself and Bo. Additionally, Marty revealed he had lost a hammer—a detail that became more significant when he mentioned hearing rumors about the murder weapon.

Despite acknowledging his struggles with anger and the stress of his marital separation, Marty wasn't considered a suspect at the time.

Marilyn Smartt, Marty's estranged wife, provided a more detailed and disturbing account of the night. She recalled returning from the bar with Marty and Bo around 11:00 PM, after which she went to bed. However, Marty and Bo later dressed in suits and sunglasses—a peculiar choice for a late-night visit to a dive bar—and returned to the establishment. This unusual attire, Marilyn speculated, could have been an attempt to establish a memorable alibi.

According to Marilyn, Marty and Bo stayed out until the bar's closing time, around 1:30 AM. However, she woke up around 2:00 AM to find them burning something in their wood stove, an action that remained unexplained, although Marty claimed it was merely a log.

In the days following the murders, Marilyn expressed to the police her suspicions about Marty's involvement, citing his odd behavior, animosity towards John Sharp, and his tendency towards violence, especially when drinking.

Complicating matters was Bo, Marty's friend and temporary housemate. A convicted felon with alleged ties to organized crime, Bo had reportedly developed an infatuation with Sue Sharp, making advances towards her on the night of the murders that were rebuffed. This rejection, coupled with Marty's hostility towards John, led to speculation that the crime could have been fueled by a drunken, rage-fueled retaliation against Sue and John.

Years later, Marilyn claimed to have discovered a bloody jacket in their basement, possibly belonging to Tina Sharp, and handed it to detectives. However, this piece of evidence was not documented in the police files, raising questions about whether it was overlooked or the entire investigation was mishandled.

In the aftermath of the Cabin 28 tragedy, the Plumas County Sheriff's Office faced criticism for their handling of the investigation, notably the delay in recognizing Tina Sharp's absence. This crucial oversight granted valuable time to her abductor.

The inquiry took another unusual turn when Marty Smartt and John Boubede, linked to the case through Marilyn Smartt's testimony, were brought in for questioning. Deviating from standard interrogation procedures, the authorities interviewed them together. This approach allowed the men to corroborate each other's stories without the usual police strategy of isolating suspects to exploit inconsistencies.

Bo's claim of being a former peace officer, easily refutable given his criminal history, surprisingly went unchallenged by the investigators. Similarly, Marty's revelations about his strained marriage, PTSD, and the mysterious disappearance of his hammer were not probed with the rigor they warranted. Both men, interviewed just once, were quickly dismissed as suspects.

Deputy Mike Gamberg later disclosed that Sheriff Doug Thomas had delegated the case to the DOJ from Sacramento. Intriguingly, the DOJ assigned detectives from the organized crime unit, not homicide experts. This decision fueled theories that Bo might have been a police informant protected by the DOJ, possibly due to his connections to organized crime.

The personal connection between Sheriff Thomas and Marty Smartt further muddied the waters, suggesting that this relationship might have influenced the leniency shown to Marty and Bo during the investigation.

Soon after the murders, both Marty and Bo left the state, with Marty moving to Oregon and Bo to Illinois, effectively closing the door on any further investigation into their potential involvement. Their deaths in the subsequent years, Bo in 1988 and Marty in 2000, sealed away any untold truths they might have known about the events in Cabin 28.

The Cabin 28 saga took a grim turn when authorities discovered three bodies but found no trace of 12-year-old Tina Sharp. This haunting absence cast a shadow over the investigation, with the FBI stepping in due to Tina's age, marking it as a potential child abduction case. Yet, despite their efforts, the trail to find Tina quickly grew cold.

Just a week after the murders, on April 22nd, 1981, Sheriff Doug Thomas expressed his diminishing hope to the Feather River Bulletin, doubting Tina's survival. The FBI, finding no leads, withdrew, leaving the DOJ to continue the search with local forces. They combed the area extensively, covering over five miles around the crime scene, but Tina remained elusive.

On April 29th, Sheriff Thomas shared a grim outlook with the press, suggesting the likelihood of Tina being found alive was fading with each passing day. Time continued to slip by—weeks turned to months, and months to years—without any sign of Tina.

Three years later, on April 22nd, 1984, Ronald Pedrini, while collecting recyclables in the woods near Feather Falls, stumbled upon a partial human skull and other remains. Initially, experts did not connect these remains to Tina or the Keddie murders, believing they might belong to an indigenous person from a bygone era.

However, an anonymous phone call to the Butte County Sheriff's Office suggested the remains could be Tina's. This call, undocumented in the case files but later discovered in a recording from 2013, prompted a re-examination of the evidence. Further investigation at the site yielded more remains, and in June 1984, a forensic pathologist confirmed them as Tina's, using dental records.

The state of the remains indicated Tina likely met her end around the same time as her family, her body abandoned in a remote area, left to the mercy of the elements for years.

The recovery of Tina's remains brought a somber closure to her family's agonizing uncertainty. She was laid to rest beside her mother and brother in a Quincy cemetery, but the questions surrounding her death persisted.

Ronald Pedrini, the man who discovered Tina's remains, remained a puzzling figure. His discovery, coinciding with the third anniversary of the murders in an isolated area, sparked speculation and rumors about his involvement.

The identity of the anonymous caller, who correctly identified Tina's remains with minimal public information, added another layer of mystery. Their precise knowledge raised questions about their connection to the case, yet the investigation at the time failed to pursue this lead, reflecting either incompetence or corruption in the handling of the case. This unresolved element contributes to the ongoing enigma surrounding the tragic events at Cabin 28.

In the early 1980s, the infamous duo of Henry Lee Lucas and Ottis Toole came under scrutiny by the Plumas County Sheriff's investigators. These men had gained notoriety in the southeast for a series of brutal murders, with Lucas convicted of 11 and Toole of 6, though they claimed responsibility for many more across the United States. Their confessions, if true, would place them among the deadliest serial killers in history.

Their potential involvement in the Keddie murders piqued interest, particularly when it was discovered that they had traveled through Northern California in 1980, just months before the tragedy in Keddie. However, this lead unraveled when it was established that both were involved in a murder in Jacksonville, Florida, on April 14th, 1981, just two days after the Keddie incident. The timeline made it implausible for them to be involved in both crimes, and they were subsequently ruled out as suspects.

Another intriguing figure was Robert Joseph Silveria Jr., later known as the "Boxcar Killer." A transient who traveled by rail, Silveria was linked to a series of murders across the country, primarily targeting individuals in homeless camps or near railway lines, often with robbery as a motive.

After his 1996 arrest, Silveria confessed to numerous crimes, including several murders, leading to his consideration as a suspect in the Keddie case. He had resided in Quincy, close to Keddie, and had multiple encounters with the Plumas County Sheriff's Office from 1979 to 1986. Silveria even confessed to the Keddie murders, but this claim was retracted when it was revealed that he was in state custody at the time for grand theft auto. He too was cleared of involvement in the Keddie murders.

A significant breakthrough emerged in 2016 when a rusted hammer was found in a pond near Keddie. This hammer, resembling the one Marty Smartt had reported missing before the murders, reignited the investigation. The hammer's discovery, decades after the crime, was a critical piece of evidence, especially since Marty Smartt had passed away in 2000.

Plumas County Sheriff Greg Hagwood, who was a teenager at the time of the murders, expressed his conviction that the hammer was intentionally hidden at the location. This finding brought renewed scrutiny on Marty Smartt as a key suspect, a sentiment echoed in a Sacramento Bee article that unearthed a previously overlooked incriminating letter from Marty to his estranged wife, Marilyn.

The letter hinted at Marty's possible guilt and resentment towards Sue Sharp, whom he believed influenced Marilyn's decision to leave him. The letter's existence and its initial dismissal by investigators were seen as indicative of the flawed handling of the case.

Further damning evidence surfaced when a counselor from the VA hospital where Marty sought treatment for mental health issues came forward in 2016. The counselor claimed Marty had confessed to the murders during a therapy session, a revelation that had been previously dismissed as hearsay.

In 2016, Sheriff Hagwood disclosed that six potential suspects were under investigation, all of whom were alive and known to the authorities. In 2018, it was revealed that DNA from the crime scene had been matched to one of these living suspects, suggesting progress in the investigation.

A pivotal piece of evidence, an envelope containing a cassette of the 1984 anonymous phone call about Tina Sharp's remains, was rediscovered in the police evidence room. This call, believed to be from someone with insider knowledge, was sent to experts for analysis.

Brenda Gerow

I n the sweltering heat of July 1980, Gerow, the eldest among her siblings, vanished into the unknown, leaving behind a trail of questions and heartache. Gerow, a young woman in the prime of her life, had been working tirelessly at a local convenience store and moonlighting as a bartender in Dracut, Massachusetts. This establishment, known for its frequent biker clientele, was one of the last places she was seen before her mysterious disappearance. Gerow's life, entwined with John "Jack" Kalhauser, her boyfriend at the time, took a fateful turn when she left with him, never to be seen by her loved ones again. Despite the distance growing between her and her family, Gerow maintained a semblance of connection, once even reaching out to her family with a promise of return—a promise that remained unfulfilled.

Her family, stricken with worry and uncertainty, fought tirelessly to find answers. They faced the daunting task of reporting her missing, a task made more difficult by the reluctance of local police to intervene, citing her status as an adult at the time of her disappearance.

The plot thickened in a tragic and horrifying way when, on April 8, 1981, a grim discovery was made in the vast, desolate expanse of the Arizona desert in Tucson, Pima County. Near the intersection of Houghton Road and Interstate 10, the lifeless body of a young white female was found, a discovery that would send ripples of horror and mystery. The body was stumbled upon by hunters, who, while driving through the desert, noticed a jacket hanging eerily from a tree. Their curiosity piqued, they investigated further, only to uncover the body lying abandoned on the harsh desert ground.

The victim, a young adult woman aged between 18 and 22 years, met a cruel and violent end. An autopsy revealed the harrowing details of her last moments—she had been strangled with a ligature, severely beaten, and subjected to sexual assault. The brutality of her murder was evident in the advanced state of decomposition of her body, which rendered her facial features unrecognizable and obscured even the color of her eyes. Yet, the forensic pathologist was able to discern certain features: she had light skin, long hair ranging in color from light brown to blond, and a distinctive white spot on one of her upper front teeth. Her stature was petite, standing between 5 feet 2 inches and 5 feet 3 inches tall, and she weighed approximately 100 to 110 pounds.

Clues about her identity were scarce. She was found clothed in denim jeans, white socks adorned with pink pom-poms, a white bra, blue underwear, brown suede shoes, and a uniquely designed blouse—dark blue with puffy reddish-colored sleeves and a floral pattern. Near her body, a denim jacket hung in the brush, as if marking the spot of this tragic scene. The desert, with its shifting sands and howling winds, may have claimed other evidence, leaving more questions than answers in this heartbreaking mystery.

In the wake of a harrowing discovery in the desert, a meticulous and exhaustive investigation ensued, painting a picture of a crime shrouded in mystery and unanswered questions. The crime scene, a desolate and haunting tableau, was meticulously documented through extensive photography. Law enforcement officials, leaving no stone unturned, even took to the skies, capturing aerial photographs in a sweeping search for any additional clues that might have been missed on the ground.

Remarkably, despite the harsh conditions of the desert and the passage of time, the decomposition of the victim's body had not progressed to the point of erasing all traces of her identity. Her fingerprints, a crucial piece of the puzzle, were successfully extracted, offering a glimmer of hope in the grim proceedings. Dental records were meticulously gathered, and in a groundbreaking development years later, DNA technology provided a new avenue for investigation. In 2006, a breakthrough occurred when a DNA profile was extracted from the victim's clothing, paving the way for the creation of a DNA profile of a potential suspect following a detailed analysis in 2007.

In a desperate bid to uncover the victim's identity, authorities initially faced a significant obstacle as they were unable to obtain fingerprints at the scene. In a dramatic and somewhat macabre turn, the victim's hands were carefully removed and sent to the FBI for analysis. This extraordinary measure bore fruit—the FBI successfully obtained fingerprints, yet the mystery deepened as they matched neither any missing persons on file nor any individuals arrested for crimes. The case was meticulously compared to several missing person cases, but all leads were met with dead ends.

Investigators scrutinized every detail, including the victim's clothing. Certain aspects of her attire led them to speculate that she might have been involved in the local county fair happening around the time of her murder. The clothing, a silent witness to her tragic end, was extensively featured on websites, National Center for Missing and Exploited Children posters, and various news reports, all in a concerted effort to identify her. Furthermore, physical evidence indicated that the victim had been moving through a wooded area before her death, as suggested by the scratches found on her body.

In an initial attempt to put a face to the unknown victim, a "crude" sketch was created and disseminated through television and newspapers. Despite this effort, recognition eluded her—no one in the area could identify her. The quest for her identity took a significant leap forward in 2012 when her body was exhumed. The victim's face was digitally reconstructed after her skull underwent a CT scan, sponsored by the National Center for Missing & Exploited Children. This reconstruction aimed to create a lifelike approximation of her facial features as they would have appeared in life.

Theories about the victim's life and the circumstances of her demise proliferated among investigators and the public alike. Some hypothesized she was a runaway in her youth, possibly estranged from her family. Others theorized that she had been murdered elsewhere and her body discarded in the desert as an afterthought. The possibility that she had hitchhiked to Tucson from a distant location was also considered. Early in the investigation, there was even speculation that she could have been a victim of the then-unidentified Golden State Killer, whose criminal activities had gradually moved southward since the mid-1970s. Each theory, while plausible, added layers of complexity to a case that seemed to defy resolution, turning it into a haunting enigma that continued to challenge and perplex those seeking justice for the unidentified victim.

In 1995, a pivotal discovery was made while authorities were building a case against John "Jack" Kalhauser for assault charges. Among his possessions, they found a haunting photograph of a young woman with light hair, gently holding a bouquet. This photograph, steeped in mystery, would later emerge as a crucial piece of evidence in a cold case that had confounded investigators for years.

Fast forward to the closing months of 2014, and the police made a startling announcement. They believed this photograph, long held in Kalhauser's possession, was connected to the enigmatic case of the Pima County Jane Doe. The woman in the photograph bore a striking resemblance to both the physical description and the digital reconstruction of Jane Doe. Intriguingly, the photograph's estimated time frame, between 1979 and 1981, aligned perfectly with the period during which Jane Doe was discovered. Kalhauser, however, remained obstinately silent, refusing all requests from authorities to identify the woman captured in the photograph.

As 2014 drew to a close, this photograph of the then-unidentified woman was released to the public, in hopes that someone, somewhere, could provide a clue to her identity. Experts noted that the background of the photograph suggested it was taken in the Eastern part of the United States, possibly at a former camping area in Tyngsboro, Massachusetts. Then, on December 23, 2014, Bill Gerow Jr., received a notification that shook the very foundations of his family's history. The police believed the woman in the photograph could be his sister, Gerow, who had mysteriously vanished in 1980 at the age of 20. Gerow's disappearance had long been a source of anguish for her family—she had left the state voluntarily with Kalhauser, her boyfriend at the time, after meeting him at a nightclub. Her departure had been abrupt, leaving her family to believe she had simply "run off." Her brother recalled a haunting phone call from her, a few weeks after her departure, from New Mexico. That call was the last time her family would ever hear from her.

Kalhauser, a figure shadowed by a sinister past, had known ties to Arizona. He was believed to have murdered his wife, Diane Van Reeth, in 1995, living under an assumed name at the time. Van Reeth's body was never found, yet Kalhauser was convicted of her murder in 1999. His criminal history was dark and extensive, including a conviction for the 1974 murder of Paul Chapman and an indictment for an attempted murder in 1979. Following his indictment for the 1979 case, Kalhauser infamously jumped bail, fleeing after being released from jail. He later married Diane Van Reeth in Nevada, using a false identity to evade capture. Kalhauser was eventually sentenced to 20 years in prison in Arizona for second-degree murder, a sentence he completed in May 2019.

In a turn of events that brought a bittersweet closure to a decades-long mystery, on September 28, 2015, it was announced that the body of the unidentified victim had been formally identified as Gerow in April 2015. This momentous identification was made through a comparison of the victim's DNA with that of her family. Her father, William Sr., expressed his incomprehension at the motive behind his daughter's tragic demise. Kalhauser was named a person of interest in her murder, with police seeking information from anyone who might have known Kalhauser and Gerow in the late 1970s or early 1980s. Following this revelation, Gerow's remains were returned to her family and cremated.

In 2017, the intertwined fates of Gerow and Van Reeth were brought to the forefront of public attention in the second episode of "Who Killed Jane Doe?" on Investigation Discovery. Gerow's brother and father gave poignant interviews, sharing their memories and the heart-wrenching impact of Gerow's disappearance and the subsequent discovery of her identity. Their stories, etched in grief and loss, shed light on the enduring mystery of Gerow's life and untimely death, leaving viewers with haunting questions about the elusive nature of truth and justice.

Bibliography

Albert, Alexa. Brothel: Mustang Ranch and Its Women. First ed., New York, 2001.

Albrektsen, Thomas. "400.000 Biler Er Blevet Undersøgt I Sagen Om Emilie Meng." TV2 East, 21 June 2017.

Bloyd, Kyle. "Police: Delphi Homicides Far from Cold Case; 18K Tips Received." WISH-TV, 16 June 2017.

Catalanello, Rebecca. "Detectives Turn to New Bethany Home for Girls in Search of Leads in Woman's 1981 Death." The Times-Picayune, 9 Feb. 2015.

Catalanello, Rebecca. "Homicide Detectives Refocus on the Man Who Found Body of 'Bossier Doe' 34 Years Ago." The Times-Picayune, 27 Mar. 2015.

Cecco, Leyland. "Canada: Unidentified Victim of Alleged Serial Killer Given Name Buffalo Woman." The Guardian, 6 Dec. 2022.

Chen, Jeremy. "Las Vegas Judge Accused of Being Improperly Involved in Double Homicide Case." KTNV.com, 3 Sept. 2020.

Egan, Leigh. "Where is Chase Massner? Veteran Disappears, Family Frantic for Answers." Crime Online, 18 Jan. 2017.

Gibson, Shane. "Man Arrested in Rebecca Contois Murder Charged with 3 More Homicides: Winnipeg Police." Global News, 1 Dec. 2022.

Guo, Jeff. "The Bonkers Seth Rich Conspiracy Theory, Explained." Vox, 24 May 2017.

Huff, Steve. "Pima County Jane Doe: Her Name Was Brenda Gerow." True Crime Wire, 30 Sept. 2015.

Identifinders International. "1981 Murdered Harris County John & Jane Doe Identified After 40 Years Leads to Discovery Their Baby, Now Age 41, is Missing." PR Newswire

Isikoff, Michael. "How a 'Slick Talker' Lobbyist Boosted the False Seth Rich

Murder Conspiracy - Before Getting Shot Himself." Yahoo News, 16 July 2019.

Kennedy, J. Michael. "Hope Dims for a Quiet Woman Who Vanished." Los Angeles Times, 14 June 1980.

Maibøll, Tinie. "Emilie Mengs Familie Beder Danskerne Om Hjælp: Fjern Plakaterne." BT.dk, 30 Dec. 2016

Maloney, J. J. "Caller Claims He Killed OC Woman." Orange County Register, 13 June 1980.

Metcalf, Victoria. "Plumas County's Keddie Murders Revisited — Part III." Lassen County Times, 12 May 2018.

Miranda, Gabriela. "Remains of Houston Couple Found in 1981 Finally Identified. But Their Child, Now 41, Is Still Missing." USA Today

Morton, Joseph. "D.C. Police, Family of Slain DNC Staffer Seth Rich Urge Anyone with Information About Murder to Come Forward." Omaha World-Herald, 4 Aug. 2016.

Murillo, Lupita. "New Technology Helping in '81 Cold Case." KVOA News NBC, 25 June 2013.

Murrillo, Lupita. "Crime Trackers: Jane Doe from 1981 Identified, Person of Interest Named." KVOA News Tucson, 28 Sept. 2015.

Olsen, Lise. "Who Killed Texas Couple Dean and Tina Clouse—and Where Is Their Baby?" The Texas Observer, 2 Mar. 2022.

Reed, Betsy. "Canadian Man Charged with Murdering Four Indigenous Women." The Guardian, Associated Press, 1 Dec. 2022.

Sandra, L. "Barry and Honey Sherman: Canada's Unsolved Billionaire Murders." The Crime Wire, 12 Jan. 2024.

Schechter, Harold. The Serial Killer Files: The Who, What, Where, How, and Why of the World's Most Terrifying Murderers. Ballantine Books, 2003.

Shapiro, Emily. "Indiana Teens' Mysterious Murders Still Unsolved 2 Months Later, Leaving Fear, Frustration in Delphi." ABC News, 13 Apr. 2017.

Tindera, Michela. "Canadian Pharmaceuticals Billionaire And Wife Found Dead In Toronto Mansion." Forbes, 15 Dec. 2017.

Torres-Cortez, Ricardo. "2 Years Later, Mother Presses for Break in Case of Daughter's Slaying." Las Vegas Sun, 26 Oct. 2018.

Truesdell, Jeff. "5 Things to Know about the Keddie Cabin Murders — and the New Hunt for the Killers." People, 22 Nov. 2016.

Truesdell, Jeff. "A Daughter's 35-Year Fight For Justice: Sheila Sharp Longs to Know Who Murdered Her Family in Their Cabin." People, 25 Nov. 2016.

Varady, Cynthia. "The Disappearance and Murder of Dorothy Jane Scott." Vocal Media.

Websleuths. "GA - Chase Massner, 26, Kennesaw." 27 Mar. 2014.

Whelan, Micheal. "The Delphi Murders." Unresolved.me, 5 May 2019.

Whelan, Michael. "The Keddie Murders." Unresolved, 27 Oct. 2019.

Willis, Carl. "Human Remains Found at Home Where Iraq War Vet Disappeared." WSB-TV 2, 2 Aug. 2017.

Wootson Jr., Cleve R. "Billionaire Philanthropists Found Dead in Basement Under Suspicious Circumstances, Police Say." The Washington Post, 17 Dec. 2017.